VARRIO WARFARE:
VIOLENCE IN THE
LATINO COMMUNITY

GABRIEL C. MORALES

TECOLOTE PUBLISHING

Seattle, WA

© 2000

® 2005, 2008, 2012, 2021

For my family, friends, and community.

May you find peace in your life!

TABLE OF CONTENTS:

PREFACE

I know of a few academic books on early Mexican-American gangs, but I don't recall ever reading any books that documented well to the basic reader the evolution of Latino street gangs from their beginnings in the late 1800s to early 1900s and to date. This work was the result of decades directly working with gangs, interviewing dozens of gang workers, and conducting my own research.

A "Gang" is often defined as a group of three or more people who interact among themselves to the exclusion of other groups, have a group name, often claim a neighborhood or territory, often use signs or symbols, and engage in criminal or anti-social behavior on a regular basis. Another definition is that "a gang exists in order to fulfill the gang members' needs: food, shelter, clothing, love, affection, identity, respect, etc." Unfortunately, some gang members confuse fear with respect and wants with needs.

American subcultures can be beautiful, a variety of music styles can sound good, different foods can taste great, but many gang members have cultural pride and gang pride mixed up. They mostly do harm to their own people; the ones they claim they are fighting for and they are proud of. Misplaced cultural pride is one reason why many kids join gangs. There is also a connection between gang affiliation and poverty, but this is no excuse. If being poor or being a minority were guarantees for being a gang member, then every kid in every Barrio or Ghetto or Chinatown would be a gang member and we know that is not the case.

On my websites, in my training classes, and in my books, I have tried to present as many issues and resources as possible for people to explore. I also often share personal stories and experiences. Some people may view this, my first book on gangs, as just another study about misguided human behavior, or examples and proof that Latinos are prone to commit violence and deal drugs. Some people in our community, gang workers included, prefer not to talk about secretive adult prison gangs. They point out that it is dangerous to glorify the gang lifestyle and that gangs often will commit even more violence after publicity. The fact is, many of our communities have been uneducated or in denial about the complex subject of gangs which is just as dangerous.

When I first started working on this book approximately 30 years ago, I initially intended to just try to help open the eyes of our community about all the harm that was being done by gang members. I have never been a cop, but I've trained thousands of cops on "Latino Culture" vs. "Gangs", all the way from fresh recruits to seasoned veterans. I interviewed and spoken candidly on this subject all the way from line officers working the trenches up to the front office brass.

I also wanted to examine the criminal justice system from prior to arrests until to the end of the prison line to improve the system. I've worked most of my career in Corrections, and I quickly become aware that most people unless they've been locked up get most of their views on jails and prisons from movies. Some movies are more realistic than others.

As stated by Edward James Olmos at the opening of his film "American Me", "This is La Vida Loca, the Crazy Life. To be silent hasn't worked". Three advisors to the movie, Ana Lizarraga, Charles Manriquez, and Rocky Luna were killed for violating the Hispanic style of "Omerta" or breaking silence. The Mexican Mafia didn't want people to see the gang depicted in such negative fashion.

Some Pachuco gangsters, like the ones depicted in the beginning of the movie, spelled the correct Spanish word of "barrio" (Hispanic neighborhoods) as "varrio" and this is the word many Hispanic gangs use today to represent their neighborhood. Many families in barrios have at least one relative locked up in the criminal justice system. According to the Los Angeles Police Department, approximately 60% of gang members will be dead or locked up in prison by the time they reach the age of 20. In some communities, gang members are responsible for as much as 80% of all crimes. Today, gangs are not just active in large urban areas, but also middle sized, and even small sized towns. They are found among all races and run across all economic levels of people. These gangs commit warfare against each other as well as commit violence against non-gang members.

So, what motivates a youngster to join a gang and be self-destructive? How do you divert youth away from negative activity and into legitimate pursuits? How do we protect ourselves as a community? This book will help answer these and other difficult questions…

INTRODUCTION

Don Antonio Velasquez was a proud hard-working man with a big thick mustache, the type worn by Emiliano Zapata, the revolutionary who fought for peasants' land rights. Antonio was born in poverty to a large traditional Mexican family in 1889 in the State of Zacatecas.

Zacatecas is located in North Central Mexico between Guadalajara on the Western Coast and Monterey on the Eastern Coast. The powerful dictator Porfirio Diaz was in control of the government. The rich got richer and the poor became poorer so the entire country was ripe for popular revolt. As the booming cannon fire grew nearer and talk of political reform in Mexico fell on deaf ears, Antonio knew he must leave his beloved country if he ever wanted to survive and provide a better life for his children.

Antonio heard from relatives about "El Norte", the wonderful land of opportunity located north of the border. The year was 1910 when he came to the United States to escape the escalating violence of the Mexican Revolution. He decided to settle in a Dallas-Fort Worth colonia or Mexican colony in the state of Texas where he had family connections.

Rumor had it that the Don moved a little bootleg-booze in order to make ends meet during the 1920s Prohibition Era. Antonio married Juanita Tamayo, a Yaqui Indian originally from the State of Sonora, who died soon after giving childbirth to the last born of their eight children. The Don and his seven boys worked long hard hours as migrant farmworkers during the Great Depression. Leaving the fields of Texas in the spring, they found agricultural work in the Mid-West. They worked the sugar beets in Idaho, picked apples in Washington at the famous Condon's Castle Orchards, traveled down through California's "Grapes of Wrath", and back to Texas for the winter.

Antonio remarried Otila "Tillie" Martinez from Lockhart, Texas, just south of Austin, and they had several children together. Around 1939, the family settled in Yakima's West Valley of Washington State. The Yakima Valley is a fertile agricultural area, very hot in the summer, cold in the winter. Yakima would be a virtual desert without the nurturing cool waters of the sweeping Yakima River.

Eventually, my great-grandfather, Don Antonio saved up enough money to buy a good chunk of land just west of Condon's Orchards. He died in 1978 leaving a legacy of "poor immigrant becomes successful American".

The Don's daughter, María de la Luz "Lucy" Velasquez-Morales de Escudero was married to Gabriel R. Morales in Dallas, Texas. Gabriel was tall, dark, and handsome. Although born to a different bloodline, he had a similar family background to Lucy. They had one son Gabriel V. Morales.

Grandma Lucy and Grandpa Gabriel with Great Uncle Charles Esparza

Gabriel R. was a straight Pachuco gangster during the late 1930s where, along with his brother Jessie, his cousin-in-law Charles Esparza, and others, was well known for sporting fine custom made Zoot Suits. They would dress up and go out on weekends to party in big cities and small towns all across the Western United States including a bar located near the corner of 1st Street and Yakima Avenue called the "First & Last". One day a bartender didn't want to serve him because he was Mexican. The bartender pointed to a sign that said, "We Reserve The Right To Refuse Service To Anyone". Grandpa Gabriel became enraged and cussed the bartender out. The bartender called the cops hoping the Yakima Police would send over a couple patrol cars. The Chief of Police got on the line with the bartender and told him, "You better serve Gabriel Morales or there is going to be a lot of trouble when all of his relatives show up!" The bartender grudgingly obliged.

While at a traditional Mexican wedding in Wapato, Washington, in 1945, a family member became intoxicated and got into a fight with the groom. The groom began to beat him severely with a crow bar to the dismay of everyone in attendance. Grandpa Gabriel would always carry a gun inside one coat pocket and a whiskey flask in the other. He pulled out his gun and ceremoniously shot the groom in retaliation.

Now looking at a felony, he fled with his young son, but was apprehended at the Idaho border. Grandma Lucy and my father were left all alone. Grandpa was sent to the Washington State Penitentiary at Walla Walla for ten hard years. When released, he paroled to Chicago, remarried, and died in 1978.

Grandpa Gabriel (Far Right) at the WA State Pen in Walla Walla, WA (late 1940s)

Tio Nico-Recent   Dad-Back in the Day

Nicolas Esparza was a young and crazy guy already on probation for getting into trouble with the law. He always hung out with Vatos Locos and his cousins during the mid to late 1950s. He also came from a very large extended family and was related to the Velasquez family. His peers would often smoke weed, drink tequila, and run the crazy streets of Yakima after school. All of them would sport their high school letterman jackets or leather jackets and cruise "The Ave." on the weekends. One day they decided to rob a near-by store just for kicks, but were soon caught by the police as they threw firecrackers out of their vehicle while celebrating their conquest. Uncle Nick took the heat for all of them and soon found himself at the Washington State Reformatory. He paroled after five years and later found work as a hairstylist like cousin Gabriel V. Later on, he became a boxing trainer in Yakima with cousin Charles Esparza Jr. and his brother Ramon as they worked with poor barrio youth to try and keep them out of trouble with the law.

Brother Joe in the mid-1970s and the Donut Shop in Downtown Seattle

Joseph V. Morales was running the downtown streets of Seattle at the age of twelve. By the time he was fourteen, he ran with a crowd of young runaways and hardcore hoodlums on Pike Street. During the 1970s, they all hung out at a well-known crime magnet called the "Doughnut Shop" on First Avenue located just across the street from the historic Pike Place Farmers Market. The Pike Street Gang's real specialty was pimping and robbing dope dealers. First, one of the guys would make a small drug deal. Later, other members of the gang would come back, weapons in hand. They would take the drug dealer's money and the drugs. What could the dealer do? Report it to the police?

After one such occasion, a very angry dealer who was ripped off spotted Joe and came after him and Joe's crime partner. Joe pulled a weapon and shot him clear through the neck. He narrowly escaped, but was later identified through a public school yearbook. Brother Joe went off to Maple Lane in the Juvenile Rehabilitation Administration for four years. Later, he did a lot more time in Seattle's King County Jail and several more years in the Washington Department of Corrections on drug convictions.

My Parents around 1960 and Me in the late 1970s with my Nephew

I was born in the poor Eastside barrio of Yakima and raised in West Seattle's High Point Projects area in the 1960s. High Point was known as one of the worst areas of the city. My Anglo mother was from a poor "Arkie" family and was once put in detention. Her only charge being "white trash out with a dirty Mexican". My father, Gabriel V., left our home and divorced my mother when I was very young. At the time, there were only a very few Hispanics living in Seattle, now there are tens of thousands, all of them coming to the Great Northwest to seek a better way of life.

It is hard to stay in school when you have constant random acts of violence all around you. At the age of five, I remember seeing a purse-snatcher get his head blown off by a little old lady with a great big gun. Bright red blood was oozing out of what used to be his head and was splattered everywhere. I ran home fast as I could to my mother totally traumatized by the incident that I had seen. I often had nightmares years after of that incident.

My mother remarried, had my sister Lara, and we were able to afford to move literally ½ block away from the projects and Forest Lawn Cemetery. We had to hustle to have any money and often my clothes were bought at the Goodwill with patches on the knees. I wore socks on my hands in the winter. Mom was on welfare for a little while and the stigma of that stuck with me for a long time. While I think she felt shame about that time period more than me, I later considered it a badge of honor.

I always had a job, even when I was young. If running away from savage guard dogs wasn't bad enough, getting robbed of my hard-earned cash after making collections on my newspaper route was worse. Later, I worked as a box boy for a Safeway grocery store and then worked the midnight shift at a local tortilla factory.

Often, I would get beat up by the Black and White kids on my way to school. Where I grew up you had to fight real good or run fast. I got pretty good at both. I trained at Joe Toro's Boxing Gym and at Javier Lopez's Karate Dojo. When school was out during the summer months, I would go stay with my relatives over in Yakima and knew many "Norteño" gangsters near the corner of 4th and "G" Streets.

Academically, school was pretty easy for me, that is, when I actually attended. I was usually bored to death with school and often under the influence. Other times, I would be too tired from my job to get up in the morning. During my sophomore year, I was absent or late a total of 42 days.

While I identified with some of the Cholos of Yakima, the 1970s breed of street gangsters who partied all day, I mostly addressed my Chicano friends simply as "Homeboys". Sometimes we addressed each other, "Hey Vato!", and the reply was usually, "Hey Loco!" This was a greeting we picked up from the older generation. You didn't jump into our inner circle, you partied in if you were accepted, and when you left our neighborhood, we had a big going away party, so literally you partied out. With the assistance of some very good mentors and the "Proyecto Saber" (Project to Know Program) of the Seattle Public School system, I graduated from Chief Sealth High School in 1978. After graduation, I enrolled in Yakima Valley Community College to study the Social Sciences and did a lot of community organizing.

My 21st birthday party was to be attended by invitation only. I was absolutely against any firearms or uninvited guests. The plan was to make it an occasion worth remembering. Man was it ever!

A liquor permit was purchased and La Cocina Popular Hall was rented at El Centro on Seattle's Beacon Hill. At first, all of the homeboys were chilling out with their ladies dancing to "Old School Grooves" which is a funky style of R & B. Soon thereafter, some hardcore Cholos from East Los Angeles came strutting in their flannel Pendleton shirts and khaki trousers looking for one of their girlfriends. Since they didn't see her, they thought they'd hang around awhile and demanded drinks. The bartender didn't know quite what to do and asked me for some assistance. I politely asked them to leave quietly and explained that it was a private party only.

They said, "Fuck off"! We own this place!" The homeboys quickly surrounded them. I responded, "You guys better leave now because my partners are getting pissed." I didn't want them there. They were ruining the good vibe!

A guy named Craig Ayers was the most vocal asking if the rowdy troublemakers needed to be bounced out of the place. The Cholos yelled, "Orale, we'll leave ése. You stay right here! We'll be back with cuetes (guns)!" I told everybody to pack up and get out of there. Brother Joe offered his place in West Seattle to go party and everybody thought that would be cool.

Joe and a couple of his partners, including Craig, went to a nearby store to get some more beer where they were ambushed by the Cholos. It was four against four, but Joe and his boys were caught without their usual weapons. The Cholos had theirs. Craig was shot through the leg and was nearly hacked to death with a meat cleaver. The Cholos got away with only a few bumps and bruises. Joe took Craig to the Harborview Medical Trauma Center. His femur bone was totally shattered so the doctors had to replace it with a steel rod.

Joe and his partners sought instant payback revenge but I talked them out of it. I pleaded with them not to handle violence with violence and to trust the criminal justice system. They told me they didn't have much faith in it and preferred "street justice" instead. I convinced them to give it a try. Mickie Perez, a friend of the family, was the only female there and the best witness to the incident. On court day, while two of the Cholos were in jail on investigation for the assault, the other two were waiting outside in City Hall Park to strike us yet again. During their escort by Court Detail Officers, one of the defendants motioned to Mickie that he was going to kill her. She was good as dead!

I told the detectives about the two Cholos outside of the County Courthouse. They just laughed. It was only a bunch of lousy Mexicans doing "Varrio Warfare"! Mickie started to have what is called "witness amnesia" and the Cholos got off the hook on the attempted murder charges. When the Cholos got out of jail, they came after me several more times. One of them called "Mosco" tried to lure me into the parking lot of a bank right in front of the cops. I knew he was armed and I was not. On another occasion, Richie who was also one of the attackers against Craig, showed up at a party near the Space Needle. He summoned a truckload of his buddies and I narrowly escaped. They shot at me twice later.

I got tired of looking over my shoulder and joined the U.S. Marine Corps. I remember at the time, a lot of people thought I was a coward and only running away from my problems. To this day, I think it was one of the best decisions I ever made. For three years out of my four year enlistment I was stationed in Southern California where "Varrio Warfare" was an everyday occurrence. Gangs called "La Rana, Big Hazard, Florencia, F-Troop, and Varrio Logan" were the names of just a few.

After my tour of duty, I worked at Folsom State Prison in Northern California. At the time, Folsom housed some of the state's most violent prison gang leaders. Built in 1880, it is a massive facility, largely built by prison labor and made out of solid granite rock. I still remember my first day of work there. As I walked down the tier, the heavy metal door slammed and echoed behind me. I saw thousands of sweating men crammed all together. The placed smelled so much of death and blood that even the use of cleaning ammonia could not cover it up.

I helped open New Folsom facility in early 1987 by transferring inmates out of the dreaded 4-A building into the new maximum security and close facility with signs posted, "No Warning Shots". Inmates with large tattoos of "Brown Pride or "Viva La Raza" were always stabbing other inmates just because they were from another neighborhood. I couldn't believe the intense violence and hatred. The California Department of Corrections was in the middle of a prison gang war in the 1980s.

One day, the Aryan Brotherhood threw a homemade bomb at me. The device was made out of a deodorant container, stuffed with matches, metal snaps for shrapnel, and treated twisted toilet paper for a fuse. I escaped serious injury but the loud echoing sound in the lockup unit was a little intimidating. On another occasion, a Black Guerrilla Family prison gang General rushed me on the tier after he felt he was issued dirty laundry. The Mexican Mafia wanted to assault me in the dining room area after they were furious at a search of their work crew for extra food items. The Nuestra Familia was trying to take over one of the yards at Folsom and the Bulldogs from Fresno were saying, "Don't worry about those guys Morales, we'll look out for you!"

I soon tired of the hostile environment at Folsom of what could be called "combat fatigue". I also got very homesick, so I moved back to Washington State to work at the Department of Adult and Juvenile Detention, better known as the King County Jail in Seattle. I was known as the "Gang Specialist" and taught Gang I.D. and Management at the Washington Criminal Justice Training Center, commonly called the Academy.

Seattle was in the middle of its own gang wars. The Crips and the Bloods had arrived as well as a local faction of the Black Gangster Disciples. The Latino street gangs from L.A. had also arrived in greater numbers. I had learned well from the veteranos that this kind of self-destructive "Varrio Warfare" had been going on for years.

This book was written in the hopes to educate people who want to try and understand the many different factors involved in gang behavior. There are no easy answers.! I do not intend for it to be an excuse on why gang members commit violence. Ten percent of profits from this book will go directly to programs that help our youth stay in school, out of trouble with the law, and help all of us as a society.

Sincerely,

- Gabriel C. Morales

Chapter 1

Gangs in America

Hispanic gangs have shown some similarities to previous groups of criminal organizations in America. Some people today forget that European-American groups had many of the same problems when they were new immigrants. Street gangs entered the recorded history of the U.S. as early as 1820 in New York City. In that year, the "Forty Thieves" gang was hired by crooked politicians to destroy ballot boxes and intimidate voters during elections. They also had a junior sub-wing called the "Little Forty Thieves". In this way, younger brothers were fostered into the gang. Other gangs were the "Plug Uglies", "Chichesters", "Shirt Tails", "Roachguards", and the "Bowery Boys" that formed within a few years thereafter. Later, the "Border Gang", "Hookers", "Buckroos", and the "Swamp Angels" evolved. Then the feared "Dead Rabbits", "Hell's Kitchen", and "5-Points Gang" came along.

Some of the early gangs were more sophisticated than others. J.H. Green describes one such organization in his 1847 book, *"The Secret Band of Brothers"* which speaks of an Aryan rother-type gang called the "Holy Brotherhood". In Article 22 of its Constitution, it directs members to "kill to get in, die to get out".1

Other groups of the same time frame, such as the "Ku Klux Klan", were highly organized.1 By the 1840s, many Irish immigrants began making themselves known as American gangsters. The Irish gangs were to become the pre-eminent ethnic group involved in criminal pursuits for the next 90 years. By the late 1880s, however, a new group began to compete with the Irish gangs.

These were the Jewish gangs, especially those Jewish immigrants who came from Eastern Europe. Some of these Jewish gangsters were guys like Edward "Monk" Eastman, who led the Eastman Gang, and Arnold "The Brain" Rothstein, who was a major figure in horse racing gambling and who conspired to fix the 1919 World Series. There was "Dutch" Schultz, who was considered a loose cannon by many mobsters, and Meyer Lansky who, although Jewish, worked the books for the Italian Mob. There was Benjamin "Bugsy" Siegel, who was also Jewish and ran with Lansky.

Siegel later recruited a fellow Jew, the extremely violent Mickey Cohen as his chief enforcer. Some elements of Murder Inc., a hire-for-kill squad, were Jewish, like Louis "Lepke" Buchalter and Abe "Kid Twist" Reles. In Detroit, the Purple Gang was mostly made up of Jewish-Americans. Jewish gangsters mostly worked with Italians, but sometimes with the Irish. It was not uncommon for gangsters of different ethnicities to change their names to dominant local ethnic groups (Joselit, 1983).

By the 1930s, they too were overshadowed by the "Black Hand" of the Sicilians and other Italian American Crime families of "La Cosa Nostra". By the end of the nineteenth century, the city of Chicago began to compete with New York in the number of street gangs. One of the first groups in Chicago, the "Market Street Gang", fostered in the "Little Hellions". If a gang became extremely powerful, it might take in a "service gang or affiliate under its wing. For example, the "Al Capone Gang" took in several subsidiaries that paid allegiance to them. Some of these were the famous "Circus Café", "Guifoyle Gang", "Druggan-Lake", and the "42'ers". They paid homage to the Capone group by providing services or carrying out orders on behalf of the gang.2

Al Capone

Two of the most corrupt politicians in Chicago were "Bathhouse" John Coughlin and his partner "Hinky Dink" Kenna of the First Ward district. This important area encompassed most of the downtown "Loop" in Chicago. It was filled with brothels and gambling houses along with many legitimate businesses. By 1911, there were over fifty major gambling operations in the First Ward alone. There were also many fine eating establishments, some owned by so-called "respected" racketeers. "Big Jim" Colosimo and his wife operated one such restaurant downtown. "Big Jim" had made a name for himself by 1919 as "Lord of the Underworld", primarily in off-track horse race betting and brothels. He was closely affiliated with the Coughlin and Kenna political machine.

One day a guy by the name of "Johnnie" Torrio, who belonged to a New York based gang, was invited by "Big Jim" to come to over to Chicago and work for his criminal outfit.

On October 18, 1919, the "National Prohibition Act" was passed to be effective January of 1920. Torrio viewed the new law as a way to make a lot of money selling liquor and beer to thirsty Chicagoans. "Big Jim" didn't really care for the idea so Torrio had him "wacked" by a young gunman from New York City named Al Capone. Torrio quickly found out that prohibition was indeed a huge windfall, but he didn't have much time to enjoy his newfound wealth. On January 25, 1925, the "Bugs Moran Gang made an attempt on Torrio's life. It was enough to scare Torrio into retirement so he handed over his entire operation to Capone, his "sotto capo" or underboss. Along with the help of his most active enforcer "Machine Gun" Jack McGurn, Capone would run the Moran gang out of town after the "Valentine's Day Massacre" of 1929.

As you can see, gangs have been a part of life in the big city even before the days of Al Capone and the Prohibition Era. Organized crime has always tried to gain favoritism from unethical politicians.

"Tammany Society", also known as the "Colombian Order", was originally a patriotic group in New York City that was later identified with the Democratic Party. Its main headquarters were located in Tammany Hall where it became a very powerful political force.

Around 1868, William Marcy Tweed was elected as the head of Tammany and began to corrupt local government officials with bribes and extortion. Tammany drew its strength on the vast new immigrant community coming to the city via Ellis Island. It continued its unethical practices for many years. In 1926, "Jimmy" Walker was elected mayor of New York City with Tammany backing. He later had to resign amidst widespread charges of corruption and racketeering.

Frankie Yale was an aspiring crime boss in the "Big Apple" when he ran afoul of Capone and was gunned down in Brooklyn in 1928. Other bosses in New York at the time were Salvatorre Marazano and Joe Messeria who were later involved in the bloody "Castellammarese War". Messeria was killed in this war by one of his own "capos", a guy by the name of Charles "Lucky" Luciano. Marzano designated himself "capo de tutti capi" or "Boss of all Bosses" and all major crime families in 1931 into "La Cosa Nostra" (LCN) or "This thing of ours".

A ruling body known as the "Commission" was set up to help prevent future wars and was run by Luciano after Marzano's death. The purpose of the commission was to resolve family disputes, approve the selection of new bosses, and to set down policy for the LCN. Capone was recognized as boss of the Chicago family. After Capone was sent to prison in 1932 and later to Alcatraz in 1934 for income tax evasion, the Chicago family known as the "Outfit" was taken over by an able crop of successors.

Among these were, Frank Nitti, Paul Ricca, Anthony Accardo, and Sam Giancana. They continued to reap enormous profits from gambling and bookmaking. The gang also became involved in taking over and corrupting unions, including some in the motion picture business. "Johnny" Roselli was sent by the "Outfit" to Los Angeles to oversee the mob's interest in Hollywood.

They also continued political graft. The Chicago Mob was very influential in getting "Jimmy" Hoffa elected as head of the powerful Teamsters Union. In 1946, New York mobster Frank Costello and Meyer Lansky sent Ben "Bugsy" Siegel to Las Vegas. Siegel got the bright idea to build a casino out in the desert (in the middle of nowhere). Gambling was legal in Nevada. Siegel felt the Mob could earn tremendous profits off this enterprise and opened up the "Flamingo Casino" on borrowed money.

Of course, the venture was not exactly an immediate success and "Bugsy" was killed at his girlfriend Virginia Hill's house up in Beverly Hills in a drive-by shooting by his mob partners. He had failed to make the interest payments on his loan. Skimming money from the casinos did eventually turn out to be very profitable for La Cosa Nostra.

In 1957, the "Five Families" of the New York LCN, the Gambino, Colombo, Genovese, Luchese, and Bonnano groups called a Commission meeting to discuss operations after the death of boss Albert Anastacia in a Manhattan barbershop and after an attempt on Frank Costello's life. Approximately eighty bosses from around the country representing virtually every major U.S. city were invited (except Seattle, which never had a recognized family). The meeting was a total disaster after state police discovered it by almost complete accident and raided the place. The media had a field day with the story of "wise guys" running amuck in the Appalachian, New York, countryside.

Regardless, the LCN continued to thrive and be involved in major crime and murders throughout the 1960s and 70s. Hoffa was convicted of manipulating union pension funds in 1967 and sentenced to the Federal Prison at Lewisburg, Pennsylvania. President Richard Nixon commuted his sentence in 1971. Hoffa wound up missing in 1975. He was believed to have been killed by the Mob. Sam Giancana was also wacked. Some said he was involved in a government plot to kill Fidel Castro and involved with the John F. Kennedy assassination.

Anthony The Ant" Spilotro was dispatched by the "Outfit" to Las Vegas. He was involved with "Lefty" Rosenthal in running mobbed up operations as was depicted in the movie *"Casino"*. Spilotro was beaten and buried by his Mafia brothers after he "got too big a head". This led many people to mistakenly believe, "They only kill their own".

John Gotti took over operations for the "Gambino" family after he had his boss, "Big Paul" Costellano, was killed in front of a popular nightspot called "Sparks Steakhouse" in New York City. Gotti's right hand man and enforcer was Sammy "The Bull" Gravano. The once "reputable" gangsters started dealing in drugs, pornography, and "snitching". It turned out they were no better than your average street scum that they talked bad about. They had lost a lot of clout from their heyday as new ethic groups took over.

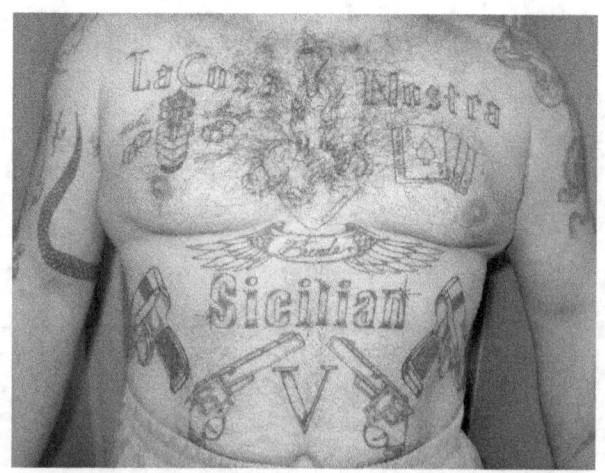

It is important to note that the Italian people, or any others for that matter, do not themselves constitute a criminal ethnic group. But, all of the different ethnic groups did have bands of individuals who were criminally involved. It was their unique experiences in America, often growing up in the poverty of inner city slums, and the common bonding of their culture that set the stage for their participation in street gangs.

There were non-White gangs in the 1800s, for instance, Chinese crime groups in Chinatown, but they rarely mixed with Whites unless there was a riot or occasionally in an opium den. Each group usually stayed in their part of town. Chinese gang involvement will be covered later in this book.

It was the same with Black gangsters and their criminal organizations; some famous ones are Stephanie "Madame Queen of Policy" St. Claire, who ran numbers rackets in Harlem, and Casper Holstein, who was her occasional rival in the 1920–1930s, and "Bumpy" Johnson who was a close associate of the Luciano crime family.

The World War I era and the 1920s saw a major expansion in industry and "blue-collar workers." The availability of jobs attracted even more African Americans from the Deep South. Between 1910 and 1930, the African American population of Chicago dramatically increased from 44,103 to 233,903. They were, for the most part, pushed into the "Black Belt" on the city's South Side.

The post-World War II era ushered in the growth of the Outlaw Motorcycle Gangs or Biker Clubs. Groups like the "Hells Angels, Bandidos, Sons of Silence, Outlaws, and Pagans" were formed.

By the early 1950s, there was hundreds of "jacket gangs" roaming around in the streets of New York City.3

Most Americans are familiar with the Broadway play and film *"West Side Story"* featuring the "Sharks" and the "Jets". What they may not know is Puerto Rican and other Latino gangs started becoming active in New York and East Coast barrios before World War II. Cuban crime groups also started operating in the U.S.

Don José Miguel Battle was the major figurehead of the Cuban "Corporation". He was a protégé of the infamous Santos Trafficante and Meyer Lansky during 1950s Mafia operations in Cuba. After the Cuban Revolution, the feared mobster Battle fled the island and set up numbers rackets on the East Coast of the United States.4

In the 1980s, the Cuban "Marielitos" arrived, the new generation of criminals trying to make it big in the U.S.A., as portrayed so violently in Brian De Palma's sensationalized film *"Scarface"* starring Al Pacino.

Drugs played a major role in the growth of the "Crips and Bloods" in South Central L.A. and other U.S. cities during the 1970s and 80s. Chinese criminal organizations called "Triads" became increasingly more active. The Japanese Crime Syndicate "Yakuza" also called the "Byorukudan", Korean Syndicates, and many Southeast Asian gangs showed their presence in America. Pacific Islander, Tongan, Samoan, and Filipino groups were also involved in crime both here and abroad.

The so-called "Russian Mafia" spread their fear in and out of their immigrant community. Nigerian and East African crime groups became involved in fraud. "Jamaican Posses" became known for their ruthless violence, especially against cops and rival politicians. Newer immigrant groups like the Dominicans and Central Americans arrived in America. As these groups rose to power a violent few of them took the place of the previous generations of European-American gangsters.

You can read more about gang history in my book *Understanding Gangs and Gang Violence in America.*

Leaders within a gang usually acquire their position based on one of two methods. Either by being the "baddest", or by possessing the most leadership skills to meet needs of the group. The gang's level of violence and reputation is often determined by the "Hard Core Element" (those most involved in illegal activity) and their ability to use the gang as a vehicle for violence to spread absolute fear in the community. The "Hard Cores", also known as "street soldiers or warriors", can eventually become leaders. They are the most violent, street wise, and are usually the most feared of the group. Retired Gangsters, Original Gangsters called "O.G.'s", or older "Shotcallers" also have a lot of influence. 5

It can be very difficult to identify a gang leader. Most gangs are in a constant state of change. The member with the most talent at any given time can be the leader. There can be the military warlord, charismatic leader, the democratic type of leader, or they may incorporate all of these elements.6

Some street and prison gangs do have a hierarchy or ranks, but such organization makes them ripe for prosecution action under the "Racketeering Influenced Corrupt Organizations Act" (RICO). Thus, many gangs shy away from any verifiable "Chain of Command" and are more horizontal in nature. 7

Except for Organized Crime, which is the highest level of gang progression, gangs are more unorganized than organized when compared to how other legal groups function. However, there is usually an informal gang hierarchy of essentially five different levels or categories of gang members. These groups are sometimes identified as: "Wanna B's/Gonna-B's" (or soon going to be gangsters), Gang Associates, Hard Core Street Gang Members, Prison Gang Members, and finally Organized Crime and Drug Cartels.

The development of gangs and transformation of members does not happen overnight, it takes years.8

Chapter 2

Gang Development in the Varrio

The first documented evidence of Mexican street gangs in Los Angeles was during the late 1800s (Dog Town) early 1900s (Alpine Street). Gang affiliations can span many generations; for example, some Hispanic gangs trace their roots to the 1930s with third or fourth generation members.

Not long after the Mexican Revolution, which took place between 1910 and 1920, a strange phenomenon began to happen in the barrios of the Southwestern United States. During this Revolution approximately one million Mexican citizens were killed. An enormous amount of bloodshed.

Another one million Mexicans fled across the U.S. border to areas where they found a culture very much like their own. These were predominately Hispanic neighborhoods, known as "barrios or colonias". These enclaves are still found even today in many cities and towns across the Southwestern States. Prior to the mid-1800s, this area was part of Mexico and rich in culture. It was sometimes referred to as "Aztlán", the mythical homeland of the original tribe that came from the Southwest which later became known as the Aztecs. In the barrio, people made tortillas, beans, and rice, which are the staples of the Mexican diet. A variety of artists, musicians, and traditional Folkloriko dances could be heard and seen.

"People would congregate at the local Catholic Church where many were baptized and given their funerals. "Yes, people could live their whole life and even die in the same barrio".1

Many couples left Mexico and crossed the Rio Grande with their young children during the Revolution. Others would decide to have children during this time so they would be born in the United States and become U.S. citizens by birthright. They settled as squatters in undeveloped areas such as "La Maravilla" in East Los Angeles. Amazed at the beauty of the area and their good fortune at getting land for cheap they shouted, "Qué Maravilla", what a marvelous wonder!2

Many of these people hoped to return to their homeland after the Revolution. Most never did.

The children of these immigrants grew up in two worlds, the Mexican and American culture. When they went to school, the American kids made fun of them. The Anglo kids made fun of them because often they had tacos or burritos in their lunch instead of sandwiches. They were severely punished by teachers if they spoke Spanish. They went to movies that often depicted American gangsters. Actors like Humphrey Bogart, Edward G. Robinson, or James Cagney were their favorites. They dressed different too. They became virtual outcasts in the mainstream culture; yet, they rejected much of their parent's culture as being too foreign in what Professor Diego Vigil calls the "Choloization" of youth. They rebelled and when you feel like you don't belong to any culture, you create your own! 3

Los Pachucos

These rebel youth called themselves "Pachucos". The origin of the word is believed to have come from Pachuca, Mexico, or El Paso, Texas, whose nickname is "Chuco". Many of the Pachucos dropped out of school and started spelling the correct Spanish word of "barrio" to "varrio". "Cálo", a hybrid dialect of Spanish and English was created. The Pachucos formed different age cliques or sub-groups that are common even today. They became known as the "heart and soul of the varrio" as they were extremely loyal and would fiercely protect their turf and reputation.4

During the 1930s through mid-1940s, the Pachucos, also called "Zoot-Suitors", could be seen in many varrios throughout the United States. The Zoot-Suitors wore wide lapels on long jackets. Pants were worn very baggy and tapered to a cuff at the bottom. "Stacey Adams" or "Florsheim" brand shoes were wing-tipped in patent leather. Sometimes "Fedora Stetson" hats were worn, as well as wide ties and thin belts. A long chain with a pocket watch attached was shown as a fashion statement. "The preferred style of music of the Pachucos was big-band swing. Songs were even made after them such as the Pachuco Boogie and dances like the Pachuco Hop".5

Many of the Pachucos were draft dodgers during World War II. If they were going to fight it would be for the turf and reputation of their varrio. While they would sometimes have a gang fight with rival varrios, they were mostly social groups. They spent most of their time partying, getting high, and chasing after their Pachuca girlfriends.

The first major public exposure of the Pachucos outside of the varrio was the "Sleepy Lagoon" murder case of José Diaz in 1942 involving the "38th Street Gang". 6

In 1943, national newspapers carried stories of Pachuco fights with U.S. serviceman. Many of these troops were upset that the Pachucos were not fighting for their country. The military, and many of the general public, felt they were "losers, slime, and a menace". The Pachucos considered the serviceman, "a bunch of squares, jarheads, and squids."

The WWII "Zoot-Suit Riots" brought an end to the era of the Pachuco as a new form of Hispanic gangster began to be seen in the varrio. 7

The Vatos Locos

The Vatos Locos (Crazy Guys) were the post-World War II generation of Hispanic street gang members. They were the Latino brand of "Rebel without a Cause" and had a James Dean look of white T-shirt, creased blue "Levi" denim jeans and black oxford shoes spit-shined like glass. "In colder weather, a black leather coat or sports letterman's jacket was worn. The Vatos Locos wore their hair short and faded or crew-cut and flat-top".8

During the 1950s, several new freeways were built in the Los Angeles area. Many of these freeways cut right through the middle of existing varrios. This served to further isolate the neighborhoods and displaced many residents who started up new cliques or gang branches such as "White Fence". Another neighborhood known as "Tortilla Flats" broke up into several different varrios. Some people also took the gang's name with them when they moved to other areas.

The INS (Immigration Naturalization Service), also known as "la migra", conducted the 1950s "Operation Bracero" which broke up even more families. The people in these neighborhoods felt very much disenfranchised with the system since they were not consulted about many of these decisions that were directly affecting their lives.

As with the Pachucos, the Vatos Locos did gang bang against rival varrios, but this usually occurred after dances and school football games or sporting events. "Music was an important part of their lifestyle. Singers and groups like Richie Valens, Brenton Wood, The Delphonics, Hannibal and the Cannibals, and Thee Midnighters were favorites. One song in particular, "Smile Now, Cry Later" by Sonny Ozuna and the Sunliners was very popular. To this day oldies are a big part of varrio culture".9

The word "Chicano" began to be used as a political identity for many young Mexican-Americans in the 1960s. A nationalist "Chicano Movement" soon gained momentum and some Chicano activist even advocated for a separate government of Aztlán. The Vatos Locos started growing their hair longer and were involved in many of the Vietnam War protests such as the "Chicano

Moratorium". During this protest a popular media personality, Ruben Salazar, was killed while covering the event. Some Vatos Locos joined radical groups like the "Brown Berets" and Varrio Warfare almost came to a halt while these gangsters were fighting the Sheriffs at "Fort Apache". The "East L.A. Riots" along Whittier Boulevard in the early 1970s was seen by many as the end of the Vato Loco era. 10

Cholos

The "Cholos" wore white tank tops or tee shirts, "Pendleton" flannel shirts, khaki pants, belts with their initials (or initial of their gang), and cheap canvas shoes known as "winos". Hair was usually worn slicked back with a hair net or bandanna. They had an oral tradition of "movidas" and legends. 11

The cholos became known for very intense turf battles across wide areas; whereas, the Pachucos and Vato Locos seldom strayed very far away from their territory. Cholos cruised deep into rival varrios and started doing drive-bys or shooting opponents from their cars. Sometimes the cholos were called "Lowriders" based on the custom lowered vehicles they drove. But it should be noted, not all lowriders were gangsters as many lowriders clubs had law-abiding and peaceful members.

There were a couple of movies that came out in the late 1970s, in particular *"Boulevard Nights"*, which depicted the crazy life of "Varrio Warfare. Later, the movie *"Colors"* came out which also portrayed Cholo-style violence based on gang wars and the work of LAPD Officer Tony "Pac-Man" Moreno Later still, the movie *"Blood In, Blood Out"* was loosely based on Robert "Moco Verde" Morrill. The rapid growth of drug usage, trafficking, and availability of weapons during this period compounded the existing problems of "Varrio Warfare" from Southern California to Northern California and beyond.12

The "1992 L.A. Riots", in the aftermath of the "Rodney King Verdicts", was depicted by the media as mostly a Black and White race conflict. In fact, many Asian small business owners and Hispanic looters, including gang members, were also involved. The damage from this riot was extensive. Over two dozen people were killed, almost one thousand people were seriously hurt or assaulted, and thousands were arrested. Well over 1,200 buildings were torched, and property damage was estimated at more than 125 million dollars.13 Meanwhile, East L.A. was virtually untouched by the riot, which was seen by many as the end of the Cholo era.

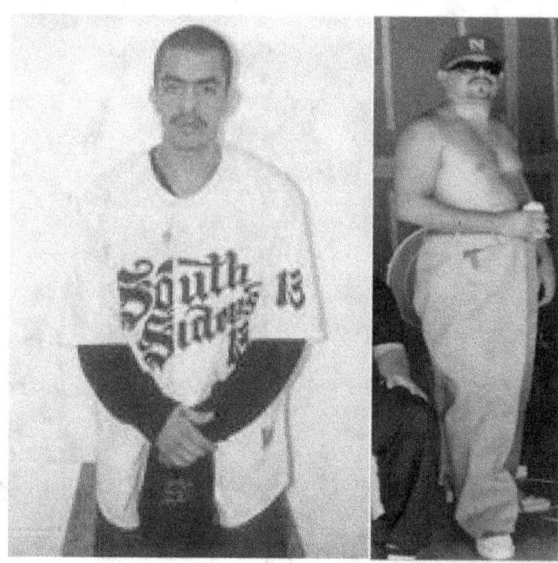

The Homies

Hispanic gang members will usually adopt a name or moniker. Nicknames for children in Hispanic families are common. Sometimes the gang will give the member his or her street name. If a kid is large, they might call him "Oso". If he's skinny, they might call him "Flaco". If he always seems happy, they'll call him "Smiley", etc. Today, most Hispanic gangsters identify each other as "Homies".

Hispanic gangsters do not dress much different now than non-Hispanic kids. The popular look is biglogo sports gear. Hats, jerseys, and coats in the gang's traditional colors. Pants were worn extra-large, baggy, and "saggin" off the buttocks. Expensive white brand name tennis shoes or brown ankle boots are standard. Body piercing and heavy tattooing is also in style today.

Larger gangs may still form different age cliques or peer sub-groups. Traditional turf oriented Hispanic gangs are now spread across the country and may even have as many non-Hispanic members as Hispanic. Drug trafficking can be, but is not always, a major source of income. The identification as "Chicano" for Mexican-Americans and "Latino" for all other Hispanic groups is common. Like the immigrant groups before them, some people from this group look to gangs as an answer to their problems. The gang is considered to be extended family. Hispanic gang members will often adorn themselves with tattoos of Aztecs, Banditos, or Gangsters. They visualize themselves as modern day criminal warriors for their race and the pride of the varrio.

Today, unlike previous generations, the urge to make war often takes the form of "net-banging". Whereas previous generations might cross-out gang graffiti or shout out a challenge to a rival, today's gangster is very likely to do this behind the safety of a computer. Many people have later died over such signs of disrespect.13

Female Gang Members

In the past, females have largely been associated with their male counterparts in such acts as holding weapons or drugs for the male members. "Pachucas, Rucas, Cholas, or Homegirls", they were sometimes voluntarily sexed in as an initiation process to become a member. Most gangs have traditionally been very sexist in that most male gang members believed it was a macho guy's job to "gang-bang" (fight) while a woman's job is to "stay home and have children".14

Sometimes the girls are tolerated within the gang for sex or to act as lookouts or to spy on rivals for the males. There may be separate female cliques who will associate with their male counterparts. Many times, fights over females are the main reason behind gang confrontations. If disrespected, the males often retaliate.15

In recent years, females in some Hispanic gangs have requested to be "beaten or jumped in" just like the males. Sometimes they have even operated as independent female gangs.16

Common names may be "Las Chicanas", "Las Locas", or "Thee Sadgirls", etc. While females still make-up only a small fraction of total gang membership, usually less than 10%, there are a few documented cases of females having strong leadership roles in male-dominated gangs.17

My experience is that during the "drug war" some females saw that their male counterparts were doing lengthy sentences in jail. They saw how the men ran the business and began to run it themselves and made a living from it. Homegirls were coming into their own, sporting gang tattoos, and are becoming more violent just as depicted in the 1990s movie-documentary "Mi Vida Loca". They often use foul language, even more so than the males. Many have been mentally and physically abused.

According to a survey of the criminal records of 100 female gang members who have been incarcerated in major urban juvenile facilities, jail, or prison, the most common felony convictions were for Drugs, Theft, TMV's, Assault, and Robbery. Females often start out their criminal careers by shoplifting with other girls or joyriding with guys. They also often start doing drugs which was their most common felony conviction, and may eventually turn to prostitution to support their habit if they remain on the streets. Most females do not stay in gangs for a lifetime, many respond quite well to counseling, and later raise families. Many times, a bulldog female or aggressive females will attempt to control the housing unit by intimidating weaker inmates and demanding sexual favors for protection. It is well known that organized crime has forced many women into the sex trade.18

Chapter 3

ORGANIZED CRIME:

LOS CARTELES

Organized Crime groups often run prostitution rings, immigrant smuggling rings, and control the dope trade. When you are speaking of "Hispanic Organized Crime", you are mainly talking about the "Drug Cartels". One U.S. official commented, "The (Italian) Mafia might well have taken lessons from this contemporary band of criminals. The Colombian organized crime groups are more prolific, better armed, and equally if not better organized."

In March of 1984, U.S. intelligence sources located the "Tranquilandia" (Tranquil Land) cocaine manufacturing plant deep inside the Colombian jungle. It had 44 buildings, six airstrips, and nine labs that produced tons of the powdery substance every month. It was only then that U.S. Drug Enforcement Agents (DEA) then realized the real extent of the problem. 1

Just weeks after the major bust, Colombian Justice Minister Rodrigo Lara-Bonilla was killed by the notorious "Medellín Cartel". The group was run by, present U.S. Federal inmate Carlos Lehder, along with José Luís Ochoa, José Gonzalo-Rodriguez, and the late Pablo Escobar. They all dealt with Mexican crime groups. Many Americans will remember Escobar's house arrest, which looked more like confinement in a luxurious mansion than a prison. He escaped anyway and was later killed after an intense manhunt. Then the "Cali Cartel" of Miguel Rodriguez-Ojeda and his brother Gilberto took over cocaine operations until their downfall.2

Relations between the region and the United States soured as the drug lords infiltrated the highest levels of government including many in the Latin American military. Drug money influenced groups on the left and right of the political spectrum even today. Nicaraguan Contras moved drugs to fund their rightist movement and some Colombian leftist groups protect clandestine drug operations and tax them.

Panama's General Manuel Noriega made a fortune looking the other way while drugs were flown in and out of his country. There were thousands of lessor known players in the dope game. To understand the role of drug cartels in Mexico one must go back decades when marijuana was discovered by the gringos.

Mexican drug lords began appearing as soon as drugs in the U.S. were first outlawed. Until 1912, products containing heroin or morphia were readily sold over-the-counter such as in the form of cough syrup. Doctors also prescribed heroin for irritable babies, bronchitis, insomnia, nervous conditions, hysteria, and menstrual cramps leading to mass addiction. Many U.S. citizens did not reach a consensus on dealing with the long-term effects of hard drug usage until the end of the 19th century when the first U.S. law restricting the distribution and use of certain drugs was finally enacted via the Harrison Narcotics Tax Act of 1914. By the time the United States entered into World War I in 1917, opiate addiction was greatly reduced but other drugs became more popular.

To the traffickers it was a matter of supply and demand and a good way to make a living. The life and death of Jesus Malverde has not been historically verified, but according to local legend in Culiacan, Sinaloa, Mexico, he was a "Robin Hood" type of bandit who was hanged by the authorities in 1909. This was just prior to the Mexican Revolution. Since Malverde's "death," he has been considered a hero to many of Sinaloa's poor highland residents; many of whom earn a living through drug trafficking. It is from many legends and real life drug traffickers like Malverde that the current Mexican drug lords have tried to also portray themselves not as villains but as heroes to the people.

The outlaw image caused Malverde to be adopted as the patron saint of the region's drug trafficking business and he was dubbed a "Narco-Santo." Malverde even has a shrine in Culiacan, Mexico, that attracts thousands of people each year. The Catholic Church does not recognize him as a saint but many of the people do. Narco-traffickers also often pray to Malverde for safe passage of their load (narcotics) to the U.S. In addition, recently many drug traffickers are praying to the image of La Santisima Muerte.

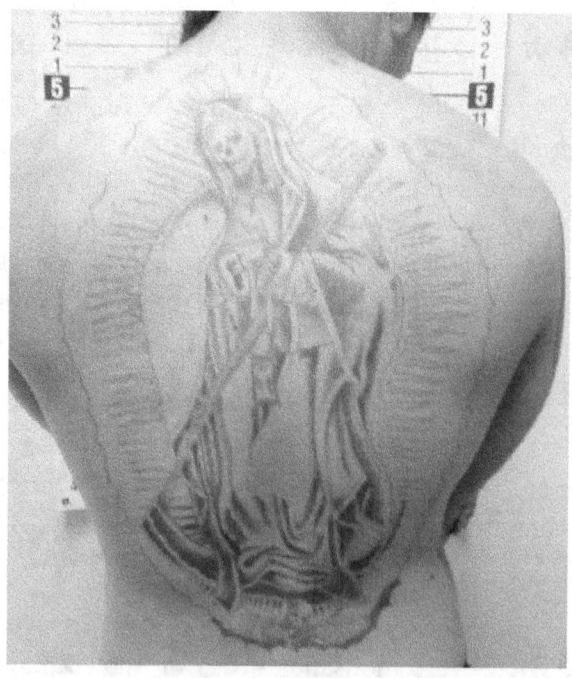

This translates into English as "The Saint of Death", but is also not recognized by the Catholic Church. Statues, Alters and other paraphernalia relating to this image are increasingly found. To understand this fairly new phenomenon read Tony Kail's book, *Santa Muerte: Mexico's Mysterious Saint of Death"*.

In the 1970s, the Mexican state government of Sinaloa launched "Operation Condor". New mega-resort hotels like the "El Cid" were being built along the state's scenic beaches. Many officials wanted to get rid of drug money in favor of expanding the resort city of Mazatlán which was expected to bring in millions of tourist dollars. They cracked down hard on crime. As a result, dozens of major drug traffickers left and headed for other parts of Mexico.3

The "Mexican Federation" was a very organized group of drug traffickers run by Miguel Angel "El Padrino" Felix-Gallardo, Ernesto Fonesca-Carrillo, Rafael Caro-Quintero and others. It consisted mainly of the "Sonoran, Tijuana, Gulf, and Juarez Cartels." Mexicans who once earned cash for transporting the Colombian's cocaine were calling their own shots.

Amado Carillo-Fuentes of the Juarez group was known as "Lord of the Skies". He got his name by flying 747's full of cocaine all over the Western Hemisphere. Carrillo-Fuentes and his drug associates even transported drugs in 18-wheeler trucks from the border to far away areas like New York City and Chicago. He died in 1997 during a plastic surgery operation in a fatal attempt to elude law enforcement. One of Carillo-Fuentes close associates, Hector Luís Palma-Salazar, was arrested in March of 1996 along with thirty-four Mexican police officers who were on the cartel payroll. But that was just the beginning. During "Operation Ghost Boat", U.S. authorities found out that even a few INS Border Patrol Agents were on the cartel's payroll.4

The Juarez Cartel was led by the Carrillo-Fuentes family. In the 1980s, Juan Jose "El Azul" Esparagoza-Morena, formerly of the Guadalajara Cartel, became involved with the Juarez Cartel and aligned with the Sinaloa Cartel. The Juarez Cartel later used Barrio Azteca prison gang members as enforcers as well as corrupt police officers called "La Linea" to fight further encroachment by Sinaloa's "Chapo" Guzman and local Juarez street gangs who worked for him. Right now, La Linea (The Line) seems to be running much of Juarez and the State of Chihuahua even though the Cartel de Sinaloa still has cells there and control of some plazas.

The Juarez Cartel became the first criminal organization in history to open up its own bank. It purchased the "Grupo Financiero de Anahuác" in 1996 for approximately 10 million U.S. dollars. In May of 1998, the Department of Justice arrested 112 people and seized over $157 million in drug assets during the "Operation Casablanca" investigation involving cartel deals in the U.S. Three major Mexican banks were suspected to be involved in the illegal transactions. 5

Juan Garcia-Obrego once headed the Gulf Cartel which smuggled drugs through Reynosa and Matamoros, Mexico, to places like Corpus Christi and Brownsville, Texas. He was arrested in January of 1996 to face charges of importing huge quantities of cocaine. His successor Osiel Cardenas was captured in 2003 after he threatened to kill U.S. law enforcement.

The Sinaloa Cartel was led by Joaquin "Chapo" Guzmán, Hector "Guero" Palma-Salazar, and Ismael "El Mayo" Zambada-Garcia. Born on April 04, 1957 in La Tuna near Culiacan, Sinaloa,

Joaquin Archivaldo "Chapo" Guzmán-Loera moved up fast in the drug world through his connections and business savvy. In the 1980s, he worked under Miguel Angel "El Padrino" Felix-Gallardo, a former Federal Judicial Police (PJF) Agent and bodyguard for the Governor of Sinaloa, Leopoldo Sanchez-Celis, and head of the most powerful drug trafficking group in Mexico.

Chapo Guzmán first escaped prison in 1993, either while hidden in a laundry cart or while dressed in a guard's uniform, and was aided by many Mexican officials. He was on the run for over ten years, hidden in plain sight, and allegedly dined frequently with high ranking Mexican police and politicians. He would show up at large parties like a celebrity, moving about the country at will with the assistance of his army of loyal followers, yet was nowhere to be found. The U.S. Department of Justice put out $5 million dollar reward for him yet nobody would touch it for fear of being killed or knowing that Chapo would pay more than that not to be found. Just to illustrate how influential and feared he was, even his rivals put out wanted posters of him.

As proof of his loyalty, Guadalajara kingpin Ignacio "Nacho" Coronel-Villareal approved of the marriage of his niece, a 2007 beauty queen winner named Emma Coronel-Aispuro, to marry Chapo soon after she won the contest. Emma was thirty-two years younger than Chapo.

Chapo was finally recaptured February 22, 2014, in Mazatlán, Sinaloa, and imprisoned only to escape yet again on July 11, 2015, out of a tunnel burrowed from the outside to under his cell at Altiplano Prison in the State of Mexico. When officials surveyed the tunnel, they found it had rails and a jerry-rigged motorcycle on it to whisk Chapo away to freedom. He was recaptured January 8, 2016, in Los Mochis, Sinaloa. During the raid, five of his security guards were killed and five were arrested. But Chapo almost made it away again when he escaped with a bodyguard and lieutenant, "Cholo Ivan" Gastelum. They fled out a trap door in the house, ran through the sewer system, popped up, carjacked an SUV, but were caught. They offered their capturers a large bribe but this time authorities couldn't be bought. Chapo was extradited a year later to the United States to stand trial and held in New York City under immense security.

Ismael "El Mayo" Zambada-Garcia was a close associate of Chapo. Mayo was born and grew up in Culiacan, Sinaloa, known as part of Mexico's "Golden Triangle" of drugs in the Sierra Madre mountain range, along with southern Chihuahua and western Durango. Mayo formed close ties to a Colombian cocaine producing organization run by twin brothers Miguel and Victor Mejia-Munera. Mayo and Chapo convinced the Columbians to continue running cocaine through Mexico.

Mayo has been a wanted man since 1998 but is very low key and uses a number of security precautions. Several relatives have been arrested, including his son Vicente in 2009 who took a deal in U.S. federal court. Mayo is still free as of 2021 and remains one of Mexico's most powerful drug lords.

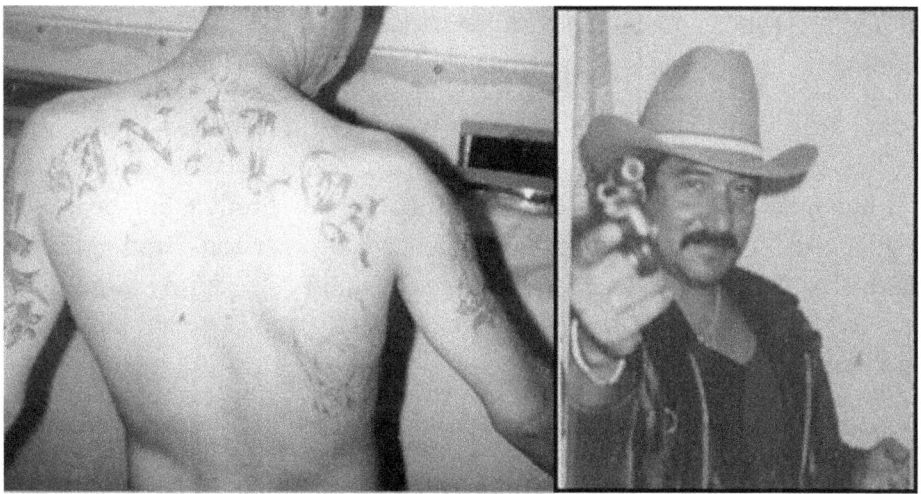

Some of the drug runners were known as "Sinaloan Cowboys" because they would fire excessive rounds into their victims and shoot up the whole place like cowboys. Today, there are at least two hundred of these gangs operating in Sinaloa and they are greatly feared for their expertise in the handling of weapons. Inside U.S. prisons many Mexican Nationals will call themselves "Border Brothers" or "Paisas". At times, the drug cartels will also contract out work to the Latino street gangs. There were also official reports of widespread threats, violence, and corruption by cartel soldiers in many of Mexico's prisons and drug rehabilitation centers. In May of 1991, a riot in a Matamoros Mexican prison left 18 prisoners dead. In August of 1993, drug gangs also rioted and took prison guards hostage.6

The Beltran-Leyva Organization (BLO), mainly made up of four brothers, was previously aligned with the Cártel de Sinaloa (CDS) before the groups went to war after the capture of Alfredo Beltrán-Leyva in early 2008. On May 8, 2008, a high ranking Comandante and Acting Commissioner of the Mexican Federal Preventative Police, Edgar Eusebio Millan-Gomez, was gunned down in Mexico City as retribution for the arrest of Alfredo. Brother Arturo was gunned down by Mexican police forces in late 2009 and brother Carlos was captured in the same year. The brothers accused Chapo Guzmán of giving information to authorities that led to their arrests and death. In 2010, a large fight between the BLO and CDS left thirty people dead. Several more killings between the two factions took place 2011-12 and brother Hector was captured in 2014.

The Tijuana Cartel, also known as the Felix-Arellano Organization (AFO), was a large family run operation that controlled the Tijuana-San Diego corridor when Mexico was carved up by their uncle, Miguel Angel Felix-Gallardo, in 1989. The Arellano brothers, namely Ramon and Benjamin, soon began recruiting San Diego area Sureño gangsters and Mexican Mafia across the border when they went to war with "Chapo" Guzman in 1992.

In May of 1993, a Tijuana Cartel hired hit squad drove around Guadalajara in search for Chapo. Totally frustrated in their efforts, they left the area and were headed back to Tijuana by plane, when they mistakenly spotted what they thought was their target at the airport. A wild shoot-out ensued and seven people were killed, including the Roman Catholic Cardinal, Juan Jesús Posadas-Ocampo. The hitmen were "30th Street Gang" members from San Diego. "Another hired gunman from San Diego, David "Popeye" Barron-Corona, had a dozen skulls, all believed to be hits, and the letter "M" for Mexican Mafia tattooed on his body. He was killed by ricocheting bullets after he made an attempt to assassinate Tijuana newspaper editor Jesus Blancornelas".7

In 1994, Tijuana drug lord Javier Felix Arellano was being transported by Federal State Police when other officers on the Tijuana Cartel payroll fired at them. There were casualties on both sides. Javier's bodyguards quickly rushed him to safety. His brother Francisco was already in prison running the family operations from the inside a Mexican prison. Brother Ramón was on the run and on the FBI's "10 Most Wanted" list until his death in 2002 during a shootout in Mazatlán while gunning for "El Chapo" when cops working for "Chapo" opened fire. Benjamin Felix-Arellano was arrested soon after in Puebla.8

Eventually, Ramon was killed by Mexican police in Mazatlán, MX, in 2002 after he was stopped for a traffic infraction. It is believed he was actively tracking down rival "Chapo" Guzman in order to kill him. Ramon was disguised, carrying a weapon, and fake Mexican Federal Police identification. Ramon drew his pistol on the traffic cop and shot him. The officer returned fire and shot Ramon as both bodies fell near each other dead. Some, including Jesus "El Rey" Zambada-Garcia, believe it was Chapo and ally "El Mayo" Zambada-Garcia who got the upper hand first, gave Mexican police logistics on Ramon and had him assassinated during the stop. Benjamin Felix-Arellano was arrested just weeks after Ramon's death by Mexican authorities and extradited to the U.S. in 2011. Some believe Chapo gave him up too.

With the downfall of Ramon and Benjamin, the TJ Cartel lost a lot of its power. Another of the younger brothers, Francisco Javier "El Tegrillo" was arrested in 2006 by the U.S. Coast Guard while on a boat in international waters approximately 16 miles off the Mexican-U.S. coast. The operation was a DEA setup by the government following a tip about a boat that Francisco Javier was buying. Authorities put a tracking device on it and waited until the boat entered international waters. It is believed that he agreed to testify against Benjamin who pled guilty and was sentenced in 2012 to twenty-five years in U.S. federal prison. Benjamin quickly surrounded himself with L.A. and San Diego area Sureño gang members as bodyguards. Meanwhile, Brother Eduardo was captured by the Mexican Army in 2008 and extradited to the U.S. in 2012 and sentenced to 15 years in federal prison.

Los Zetas were once aligned with the Gulf Cartel and the AFO/Tijuana Cartel against Chapo Guzmán and the Sinaloa Cartel. They were started by Arturo "Z-1" Guzmán-Decena who was an elite former military officer in the Mexican Army Airmobile Group of Special Forces (GAFE) that were roughly the equivalent of U.S. Army Green Berets. Original Zetas members were trained in the U.S. by American Special Forces trainers. In their early days, Zetas also allegedly worked with Guatemalan Special Forces called "Kaibiles" and were known to have several training camps.

On November 21, 2002, Z-1 Guzmán-Decena was gunned down and killed by the Mexican Army in the border city of Matamoros, Tamaulipas. After the death of Z-1, the next Zeta leader to take over was Heriberto "Z-3" Lazcano-Lazcano who was a former GAFE like Z-1. The low profile Lazcano-Lazcano was killed in 2012 near Progreso, Coahuila, by the Mexican military. Many believe that a high profile #2 Zeta at the time with greater aspirations, Miguel "Z-40" Treviño-Morales, gave Z-3 up to authorities.

While the initial Zetas core group were former military, most are now either dead or in custody. "Zetitas" with no prior military experience were often recruited from gangs or poor youngsters who were hungry to make good money working for the expanding cartel. Unlike the original founders, Z-40 Treviño-Morales had no military experience, and instead worked for a local gang as a teenager before being recruited in the 1990s to work for the Gulf Cartel. He was known by his adversaries and law enforcement officials for his violent reputation as a "brutal assassin" responsible for being behind much of the cartel violence in Mexico at that time.

Z-40 was captured July of 2013 outside of Nuevo Laredo and now occupies the same high security cell that once housed Chapo prior to his escape. Z-40's brother, Omar/"Z-42", took over on the streets for a short time period but was captured in March 2015. Intelligence indicates that both brothers continue to operate the group from within the prison via brothers Juan Francsico and Rogelio "El Kelin/Z-2" Gonzalez-Pizana who led the Zetas Unidos faction. Some intelligence says orders are now received by nephew José Francisco "Kiko" Treviño while others say the new overall leader is Francisco Javier "Pancho" Hernandez Garcia, or Sergio Ricardo "El Grande" Basurto-Pena, and Maxiel "El Contador" Barahiona-Nadales.

The Cártel del Noroeste (CDN) are "New Breed Zetas" and at war with "Vieja Escuela Z" (Old School Zetas) who are allied with Grupo Bravo in Nuevo Laredo and Tamaulipas, in northeastern Mexico. La Vieja Escuela operate out of the Matamoros area and are aligned with the Gulf Cartel as the Zetas were originally. Old School Zetas fight the Cártel Jalisco Nueva Generacion (CJNG).

The Guadalajara Cartel in the State of Jalisco, MX, was led by Ignacio "El Nacho" Coronel-Villareal who was aligned with the Sinaloa Cartel and Chapo Guzmán. Nacho first began to learn the drug trade under Amado Carrillo-Fuentes and the Juarez Cartel in the 1980s. But after Amado's death he aligned with Luis Valencia-Valencia and Cartel del Milenio in Jalisco and with the Beltran-Leyva Organization in Sinaloa. When the BLO broke off from the Sinaloa Cartel alliance, Nacho backed up Chapo Guzmán and moved tons of cocaine into the U.S. as well as becoming known as the "King of Crystal" (Meth). On July 29, 2010, Coronel-Villareal was killed in a shootout with the Mexican Army which opened up a big power vacuum in Jalisco by Nemesio "El Mencho" Oseguera-Cervantes who founded the Cártel Jalisco Nueva Generacion (CJNG).

Although he was born in Aguililla, Michoacan, "El Mencho" spent part of his early life living in the United States. He was arrested a couple of times in California and did a few years in a federal prison in Texas. He was deported to Mexico in the 1980s and at one time was a police officer in Jalisco. While not well educated, having dropped out in Primaria (Elementary) school, Mencho learned how to survive well in the world of drugs. He started working for the Milenio Cartel as a Sicario (Assassin) using skills he learned in the U.S. and as a policeman to gain intelligence.

While cartel leaders like Chapo Guzmán preferred to buy loyalty and protection from government officials, Mencho made a name for himself by taking government forces head on with several aggressive attacks and shows of force spread on the internet via video. He also expanded his territory by taking on Zetas and Knights Templar and soon controlled most of Jalisco, Colima, and Guanajuato, as well as parts of Michoacan. His main product was selling methamphetamine.

Chief Adrian Carrera-Fuentes was previously sentenced to six years in prison for his part in money laundering schemes he received on behalf of the cartels. He headed the Mexican Federal Department's Anti-Drug Unit from 1992-93. The corruption continued to the highest levels of government. Former Mexican Government Drug Policy Chief, General Jesus Gutierrez Rebollo, was on Carrillo-Fuentes' drug payroll. He was arrested in February of 1997, and later sentenced to 13 years plus for his role in drug trafficking operations. Rebollo was the highest-ranking Mexican government official to date to be tried on corruption charges.9

Raúl Salinas de Gotari, the brother of a former Mexican President, had strong ties to drug smugglers. In January of 1999, he was given a sentence of fifty years, later cut in half by an appeals court, for his role in the assassination of José Francisco Ruiz Massieu who was the number two official at the time of the Partido Revolucionario Institucionál (PRI). Mexicans applauded Mexican President Vicente Fox's efforts and following President Felipe Calderon's even greater efforts to the attack the drug corruption problem. Many wondered how far he would succeed and if all the bloodshed was worth it?

The Federal "Southwest Border Initiative" started as an integrated response to the growing drug trafficking problems between the Mexico and U.S. It tracks sophisticated cartel smuggling operations and violence along the border area. Dr. Julio Amador, a former Tijuana, Baja California forensics expert, has seen his share of cartel homicides. "I do not believe the United States can win the drug war given the present economic conditions in my country". Some people stated Mexico needed another revolution to clean the country up, but experts projected that Mexican immigration of the last century would pale compared to the numbers who would cross the border in a new conflict.

If police get in the way, smugglers will not hesitate to kill them too. There is a saying in Mexico, "Plata or Plomo?" (Silver or Lead?) If they can't bribe cops, they will eliminate them. DEA Agent Enrique Camarena was trying to put a stop to the funneling of drugs into the U.S. when he was kidnapped, tortured, and executed by the Sonoran Cartel in 1985. His death was an indication of just how bold the Federation had become. Tijuana Police Chief José Fredrico Benitez was killed after he promised to make reforms. The body of Jorge Garcia-Vargas, a Commander of the National Anti-Narcotics Institute was found along with three of his bodyguards in September of 1996. On January 3, 1997, Hodín Gutierrez, a young prosecutor who had investigated the Benitez killing was shot 120 times by four men carrying AK-47's. The Arellano-Felix Tijuana Cartel was believed to be behind the cold-blooded murders. Since then, groups like Los Zetas, a renegade faction of Mexican Special Forces have murdered thousands of people. The violence weighed heavily in the 2012 Mexican Presidential elections.

The cycle of violence in Mexico crossed over into the United States. Warring factions of the Ramos and Mendoza drug dealing families have clashed for decades. Deaths numbered more than fifty starting in San Francisco in 1988, when a high ranking member of the Mendoza family had his car riddled with bullets. A year later in Michoacan, Mexico, six members of the Mendoza clan were shot and killed. The blood feud continued all the way to the little town of Sunnyside, Washington, where more violence broke out years later.10

These drug networks were spread all over the United States. Cartels found families were a much safer way than gangs to deal drugs. Most close family members would never rat out a relative while gang members roll over and become law enforcement snitches on a frequent basis. Thus, it is generally harder to convict family members. On September 17, 1998, eighteen people were massacred in a small village outside of Ensenada, Baja California, women and children included, as a message from the drug lords.

One of the dead victims, Fermín Castro, was known as the "Iceman", a "narcotrafficante" who made frequent trips to Arizona and Nevada. Even by cartel standards it was a brutal crime scene. Drug Cartel expert Steve Duncan states, "These cartels use prison gang members as executioners. New alliances are being created endangering our nation's safety. Cross-border violence has increased as the violent nature of the cartels increase. It grows more violent each day and it is not just gang members. It is a generation of young men in Mexico who obtain pleasure in torturing, killing, and mutilating their own people!" 11

Many Americans, including California Senator Diane Feinstein, wondered if we could trust the Mexican Government since very few of the drug kingpins were extradited to the U.S.

Chapter 4

PRISON GANGS:

LA PINTA

When a person is arrested on criminal charges, they will often sit out their time in jail if they cannot bail out or get a personal recognizance release pending court. If they are sentenced to jail, most will not do more than a year locked up. While there are gang members in jails, it is generally harder for them to get organized there since there is more restrictive movement. There are also more limits on personal property in jail, and less contraband, which can be a main cause for inmate violence.

Inmates doing prison terms will usually do more than a one-year sentence. For more serious crimes they may even be doing a "life sentence", thus, they can get more organized. Whether in jails or prison, Correctional Officers (C/O's) attempt to keep warring gangs away from each other. This is not always an easy task.

A general daily routine for an inmate is to get up at approximately six in the morning for breakfast and get ready for work, school, or court. Counts are taken throughout the day in order to prevent escapes and for inmate safety reasons. Those inmates not enrolled in programs usually go back to sleep. Some may go to recreational yard, speak to their attorneys and do legal work, or get family visits. Lunch is served by noon and inmates usually return to their cells or get a sack lunch. Those who have afternoon programs or recreation do so. They might play dominoes, cards, or outdoor sports. Some prisons also allow weightlifting. Dinner is served by six and most watch TV, if allowed, then finally call it a day. The routine is usually extremely boring except for the occasional fights.

Corrections Officers dislike the word "Guard" as it implies that they are "just guarding the prisoner" when in actuality they do much more. Some have started using the title "Correctional

Peace Officer" since they try to keep the peace inside the facility. They are in essence "prison or jail cops", but may also serve as crisis counselors or advisors and may wear other hats as they perform their duties.

Gangs in prison originally started as protection groups from other prison gangs and to act as a welcoming committee for new prisoners after their intake into the system. Prison gangs are often classified as "Security Threat Groups" in correctional facilities because they tend to disrupt the security and normal operations of a facility. This term includes other organizations that are "Disruptive Groups", but not normally associated with outside street gangs. Nationally, it is believed that there are at least 283 different prison gangs.1

Prison gangs are much more violent than street gangs. From 1970 to 1980, one hundred eighty-nine inmates were killed behind prison walls in the California Department of Corrections, the vast majority of them by prison gangs.2

Street gangs and prison gangs are closely intertwined today with the "revolving door" of the criminal justice system. Street gang members are groomed by prison gang members to "put in work, make their bones, and earn their stripes". If a street gang member is "courted in", he will have to prove himself out on the yard.

According to some California prison gang experts, "They have three things in common: Control, drugs, and power. All of them have a blood oath. Once you're in, you're in 'till death!" Once a prison gang member returns to the street, they are expected to collect taxes for the gang and kickback money or drugs to their brothers behind bars. If they do not do so, they may be "checked" or killed.

Mexican Mafia

Also known as "La EME", this prison gang began in the very late 1950s at the Deuel Vocational Institute in Tracy, California. The group was originally known as the "Baby Mafia" and built its infrastructure based upon the Cosa Nostra. The object of this group was to protect the Chicano inmates from other groups, to control criminal enterprises within prison, and later to control the action in the varrios. By the early 1970s, the gang struck an alliance with the Aryan Brotherhood.

Gangs that participate in Mexican Mafia (EME) politics and put in work for the prison gang on and off the streets are given a "red light". They are not to be assaulted. Gang members who do not kick back drug profits to the gang or do not take care of business are given a "green light" and their names are "put into the hat" to be assaulted on the streets, in jail, or in prison. The EME is a "Blood in, Blood out" organization, meaning you often have to kill to get in and will die to get out. Unfortunately, it has an ample number of young Chicanos ready to join.3

Members are called "Carnales" or brothers of the family. Close Associates are called "Camaradas". Those who made weapons and were known as killers became the gang's enforcers. Non-affiliated inmates were forced to pay rent to La EME for a prison cell that the state owned. Members who had skills at bookkeeping or running a commissary store from their cells became the "money men". Money could be cigarettes, money orders placed on inmate's books, or something as simple as Top Ramen.

Prison investigators have found that some members have thousands of dollars on their books. The introduction of contraband and the smuggling of drugs into prison were other major gang activities.

EME members were known for being well groomed with clean cells so they would not catch as much heat from the officers. Gang discipline was enforced through "the holding of court". If determined guilty of a major violation or disrespect, the person's name was put on a hit list. One of the group's early leaders was Rudolfo "Cheyenne" Cadena. The movie *"American Me"* filmed in East L.A., Chino, and Folsom Prison was based on his life. Also, shown in this movie was the character "J.D." depicting Joe "Pegleg" Morgan, the alleged "Godfather" of the Mexican Mafia for over twenty years.

While based on the true story of the Mexican Mafia, several parts were fictitious including showing the killing of Santana (Cadena) by his own gang. The EME also did not like the sodomy scenes. Another movie *"Blood In, Blood Out"* directed by Jimmy Santiago Baca depicted a similar story but omitted the true historical nature of gang alliances.

The EME was so secretive that most prison staff did not even know they existed. The first public mention of the group was in 1968 when San Quentin Warden Louis S. Nelson stated that his staff had "eliminated the Mexican Mafia". While the department had in fact isolated many of the troublemakers in segregation, the group was firmly entrenched and others quickly stepped in to fill the void. 4

Eventually, the EME began using the number "13" as a symbol for their organization. This symbolized the thirteenth letter of the alphabet "M", or "EME" in Spanish. The main rag color used by the group is blue. The EME's main recruitment area was the SUR or Southern California varrios. By the mid-60s, the prison gang made many enemies of former EME members and "Farmeros" from Northern California. In 1968, the "Nuestra Familia" (Our Family) emerged as a self-protection prison group after a dispute arose when an influential EME member stole another inmate's shoes. The victim was from Northern California. Many violent assaults occurred between NF and EME as both struggled for power.

A truce occurred and a meeting was organized. At this December 1972 meeting Cadena was killed at Chino Prison's Palm Hall by the Nuestra Familia which resulted in a continued bloody war.

In 1977, there was a federal prosecution of several high ranking EME members including "Blackie" Segura, Robert "Robot" Salas, and Adolf "Champ" Reynoso. The trial focused on the criminal exploits of the gang, bank robbery, and the gang's involvement with "Community Concern", in the federallyfunded "Project Get Going", and EME influence over L.A. rehabilitation facilities was also examined. One of the government witnesses, Ellen Delia, was murdered while en route to the capitol in Sacramento to testify. The larger story of this incident is told in Robert Morrill's book, *"The Traffic Stop".*

The "Father's Day Massacre" in 1982 at Folsom was just another one of the prison gang wars and again showed the administration the violent disruption of the gangs as the EME battled the Black Guerrilla Family. Eleven shots were fired with one of the tower officer's bullets striking and killing an EME soldier. Six Black inmates were stabbed in the melee. The prison went on immediate lockdown and was taken off gradually to prevent further violence but the gangs had no intention of stopping.

In 1984, one hundred and eight inmates were stabbed. Six died. In 1985, two hundred and sixteen were stabbed and seven died. Finally in 1986, a truce was called between the two warring gangs and the violence ebbed for a while. 5

Veteran officers would say the prison yard would be very eerie with almost total silence just before it erupted into total mayhem. Sometimes victims were former EME members when the gang "cleaned house". Nico Velasquez was an EME leader who was killed by his cellie in Tehachapi. He got in trouble for arranging a truce with the Black inmates at Folsom. "Moe" Ferrel was a well-liked EME member who also fell out of favor and was stabbed repeatedly on the tier at Folsom.

Moe survived and was sent to the U.C. Davis Medical Center where he abruptly proceeded to pull out his life-support system. He knew that he would live the rest of his life in grave fear that the EME would finish him off. Another vicious EME hitman once housed at Folsom and also part of the truce, Ernest "Kilroy" Roybal, dropped out of the gang and became "reborn". Sal Buenostro was stabbed 30 times in the L.A. County Jail right in front of Sheriff's Deputies, allegedly for disrespecting Joe Morgan and for not making a phone call for his Mafia brothers. Two EME leaders, Benjamin "Topo" Peters and Rene "Boxer" Enriquez, smuggled in handcuff keys in order to free themselves to attack. When they were done with him, they were re-cuffed by Custody Officers, but were not fazed at all by their brazen attack.

Anthony "Dido" Moreno was a former EME member who had disassociated himself from the gang way back in 1983, but was still involved in criminal activities. On April 22, 1995, Morena was killed for by Sangra street gang members for violating the code of lifetime membership. Four members of his family, including two children, were also killed. During the executions an EME code violation occurred by the hitmen's vicious act of killing innocent children. One was killed by La EME on Death Row.

After the L.A. Riots, numerous meetings were held in 1993 with the various EME aligned street gangs via Peter "Sana' Ojeda with the approval of Joe Morgan. An order was given to stop drive-by shootings. They were told to walk up to handle any "beefs" or disputes face to face. The EME greatly intensified its control over Southern California and ordered the SUR 13 gangs to have no Black members.

Three main objectives were: stop drive-bys and invoke walk-ups, take over the L.A. County Jail, and to further tax SUR 13 street gangs or "green light" them. More meetings were held in Southern California parks and hotel rooms, some of which were recorded by law enforcement. The gang's lack of finances led one former member to label the group the "Welfare Mafia".

In September of 1996, the EME and SUR 13 sympathizers attacked members of the Black Guerrilla Family and African- American gang sympathizers at New Folsom, now called CSP-Sacramento County. "One inmate was killed, four suffered gunshot wounds, and six received stab wounds. Officers tried breaking up the disturbance with rubber bullets and, after inmates still refused orders to stop, used live rounds." Twenty-one shots were fired, 56 inmate manufactured weapons were recovered after the incident. The long prison war continued. 6

The first phase of RICO trials against more EME finished in September of 1997. During the trial, evidence showed several high-ranking EME leaders on videotape organizing and plotting new crimes. One defendant with Mexican Mafia connections, Ernest "Chuco" Castro rolled over on his former brothers at the highly publicized trial. Nineteen EME members, including many of the top leaders of the gang, were convicted and given long prison sentences. One was murdered before trial and the only one who was acquitted in the trial, Victorio Murrillo, was murdered on EME orders.

Another phase of EME trials finished in September, 2000, against forty other members and associates resulted in convictions, including Sally Peters, wife of the longtime EME shotcaller "Topo" Peters who died in prison in February, 2001. Topo, Ruben "Tupie" Hernandez, and Thomas "Wino" Grajeda all represented warring EME factions at the time. Rene "Boxer" Enriquez backed the Topo faction and also became embroiled in prison gang feuds. He eventually dropped out and his story can be read in Chris Blatchford's book, *The Black Hand"*.

In January of 2005, federal, state, and local law enforcement conducted "Operation La Mano Negra" which resulted in multiple Mexican Mafia arrest of members such as Richard "Cheeks" Buchanan (C-26365). Multiple associates and even correctional staff were caught up in the case. Longtime EME member and Orange County shotcaller Pete "Sana" Ojeda (B-30052) was arrested in June, 2005, during "Operation Nemesis".

In June, 2006, more San Diego EME, associates, and street gang members were arrested in "Operation in The Hat". Long respected EME Carnal Richard "Gato" Martinez and the younger Raul "Huero-Sherm" Leon were caught up in that swoop. Also, in 2006, Ruben "Night Owl" Castro of 18th Street was indicted on a new RICO case because of criminal operations he ran from, what is supposed to be, the most secure prison in America.

In April, 2007, law enforcement cracked down on a crime ring run by "Pee Wee" Aguirre's little brother Richard "Psycho" Aguirre. Their Mom was also arrested.

Operation "Del Sol" was a November, 2008, bust named after the local varrio that "Bat" Marquez claims. Del Sol member Dario Martinez was killed by San Diego PD on August 7, 2007. The gang vowed revenge for his death and stepped up activity. On November 1, 2011, Bat was sentenced to Life Without Parole in the BOP. Bat finally put a "Black Hand" with blood signifying all his kills on his neck. Today, he is considered a major player in the BOP.

In 2009, authorities launched "Operation Keys to the City" against San Diego County gang members with ties to La EME. Mauricio "Cyco" Mendez was sentenced to 26 years but deemed no good in BOP.

2009's "Operation Keys to the City" out of San Diego locked up more EME and their supporters. By 2010, the BOP only listed fifty Mexican Mafia members from California, but they controlled an estimated 2,500+ hard core Sureños. As stated before, "Old Rube" Soto and "Champ" Reynoso still had a lot of clout in the BOP at the time this book went to print. In CDCR, the picture is constantly changing, but several EME continue to wield considerable power behind the walls and out on the street.

Since then, several more RICO's have taken place, yet the gang continues to terrorize jails, prisons, and the community.

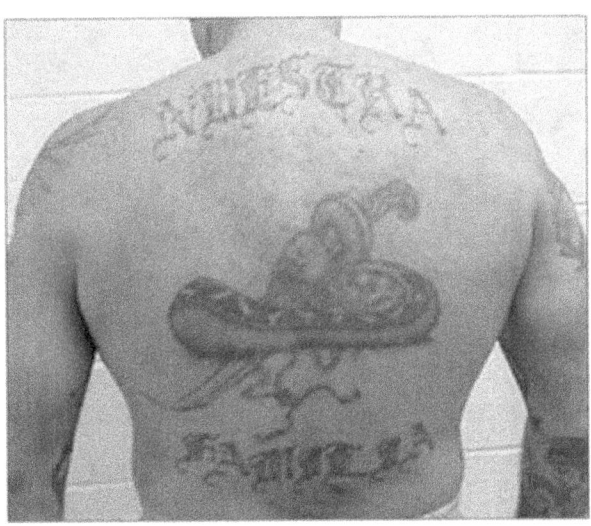

Nuestra Familia

Originally called "La Nuestra Familia Mexicana" in the mid-1960s, the Mexican part of the name was later dropped as they started to recruit non-Mexicans. The Nuestra Familia was a highly organized paramilitary group with a written Constitution, secret NF schools, and originally had some anti-government elements who aligned with Blacks. One popular book that was read by the NF was an old Chinese manuscript "Sun Tzu: The Art of War". It states, "It will not do for the army to act without knowing the opponent's condition, and to know the opponent's condition is impossible without espionage. Like other prison gangs, they have a "Blood In, Blood Out" oath. The NF even operated prison gang bank funds to further its causes. The Nuestra Familia official color is red, their song "El Corrido de Nuestra Familia". Later, they chose the symbol of the Roman numeral "XIV" to represent the fourteenth letter.

Robert "Babo" Sosa was chosen as their first elected General but was impeached for using heroin and lack of leadership during the "Black Bob-Brown Bob War" against him. In 1982, over twenty members, including Robert "Black Bob" Vasquez, a member of the ruling council, were indicted in Fresno by RICO statute as being involved in a criminally run organization. They were found guilty in 1986.

After 1980, the basic NF recruitment area is in Northern California varrios from the Bay Area to Fresno and to the Sacramento area to Delano, CA, in what was sometimes called Nuestra Raza or the Northern Structure. The NR/NS was disbanded in 197 and the NF then recruited from Norteno Soldados (N-SOLS). They are known for taking detailed notes on allies, enemies, and officers. They are organized into squads and may wear symbols to show rank or categories, stars for hits, and "huelga" birds for NR teachers who school new recruits. Prospective members must prove themselves worthy to be in the prison gang. They are put on probation and must undergo strict training called the "14 Bonds". Penalties for not following the code could be extra push-ups or could be death.

The NF has an oath:

"If I lead, follow me

If I hesitate, push me

If they (EME/SUR) kill me, avenge me

If I am a traitor, kill me!"

In 1992, another high-profile RICO trial of the NF leadership was held in San Jose, California. In 3,600 pages, the grand jury indictment stated that the gang had continued its covert activities both inside prison and out on the street.7

Twenty-one members were charged with committing nearly one hundred different felony acts, including six killings in the San Jose area after several members were paroled in 1990. Gang leaders ordered many of the killings and some named in the case never left their prison and jail cells.8

Louie Chavez, a former NF member, agreed to testify for the prosecution stating, "I was tired. Tired of them killing a lot of good homeboys for no reason." The trials demystified prison gangs as violent predatory groups who were now in disarray.

In 2001, another RICO indictment was handed down against twenty-one members of the NF after "Operation Black Widow". All eventually pled guilty and many of the leaders were incarcerated in the Federal ADX at Florence, Colorado.

The following incident happened at New Folsom Prison in 1989: "Two Northern Structure soldiers went to the weight pile area and received two metal shanks (homemade knives) from a Black inmate who had concealed them in a newspaper. They waited for yard recall to the housing units and, as three SUR 13 inmates were about to enter a sallyport that was known as "Blood Alley", ambushed the unsuspecting victims and stabbed them repeatedly right in the blind spot underneath of the main Central Yard gun tower." The two Norteño soldiers had earned a trip to the Security Housing Unit (SHU) and they had earned themselves a promotion within the structure known as Nuestra Raza.

Texas Syndicate

The Texas Syndicate (TS) formed at San Quentin and Folsom Prisons during the early 1970s. An official logo or "Copia" was drawn up made of a "T" superimposed with an "S". The TS had a strict set of rules. Its nucleus was made up largely of inmates from Texas who were incarcerated in the California Department of Corrections (CDC). While the TS prison gang was small, they were the most feared on the yard because of their propensity for violence and ruthless assaults. When released, many TS members returned to their home state of Texas. The TS expanded rapidly in the Texas Department of Corrections (TDC) after the "Estelle vs. Ruíz Lawsuit" that dismantled the state's old inmate boss trustee system. Between 1984 and 1985, there were fifty-two gang related deaths, many attributed to the Texas Syndicate. Today, they are still considered a serious security threat in Texas but are almost unheard of now in California.

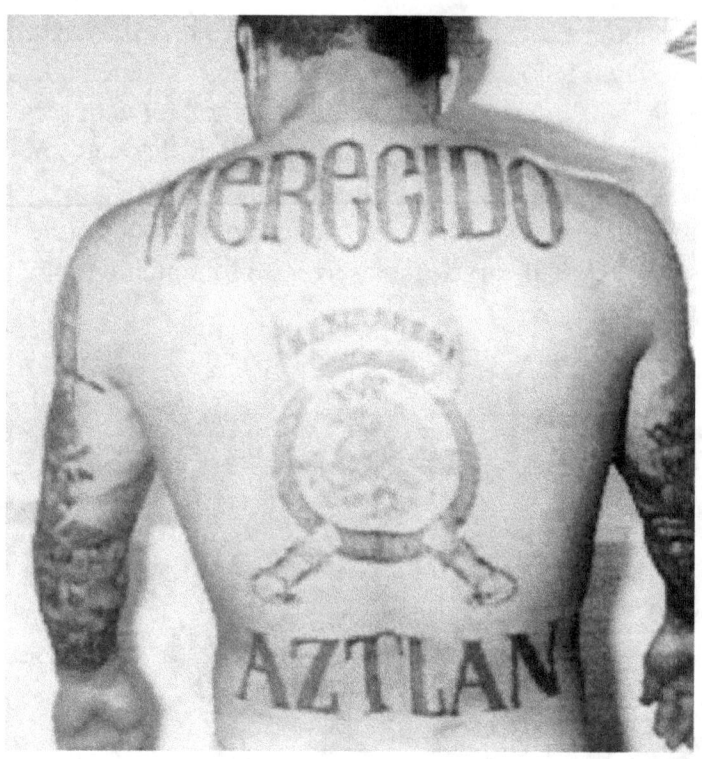

Mexikanemi

This group, also known as the "Texas Mexican Mafia", was based on the California EME and was founded in the early 1980s. It was started by inmates opposed to the leadership and ideas of the intensely hated Texas Syndicate. The Mexikanemi Constitution written by founder and President "Herb" Huerta states, "In being with a criminal organization, we will function in any respect or criminal interest for the benefit or advancement of La EME. We will traffic in drugs, contracts of assassinations, prostitution, robbery of high magnitude, and anything we can imagine!" 9

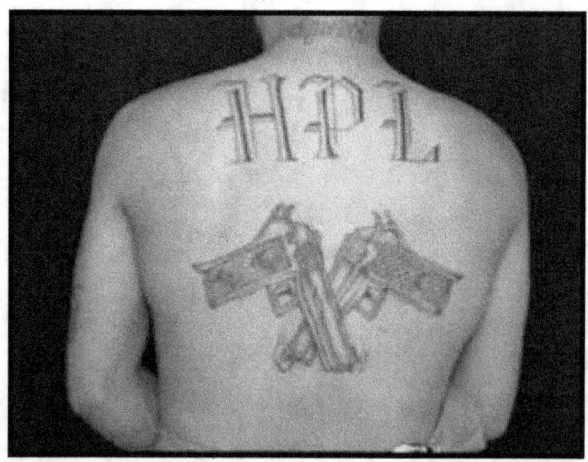

Los Hermanos de Pistoleros Latinos

HPL is a Hispanic prison gang founded by Joe Mendoza and Alberto Rodriguez in Texas during the late 1980s. The Spanish translation of the gang's name is "Brotherhood of Latin Gunmen." It operates in most prisons and on the streets in many communities in Texas, particularly Laredo.

A Texas inmate named Alfredo "Chino" Avitia founded the HPL in the mid 1980's within TDCJ. Avitia later appointed Jorge "Gato" Soto as his successor when he (Avitia) paroled. Due to serious internal problems such as rank appointments and recruitment, Soto and Gregorio "Goyo" Lopez had a dispute which caused a split. Soto's followers became known as 45's/Los Fieles and Lopez' followers as 16-12's/Los Verdaderos. The Pistoleros Latinos began to multiply in the 1990's after the gang began recruiting members from cities outside of the Rio Grande Valley. The original HPL members from the Rio Grande Valley resented the new members being recruited from San Antonio and Houston, Texas. The HPL remained low profile until 1999 when both the factions reunited. Officials estimate there are about 1,000 HPL today.

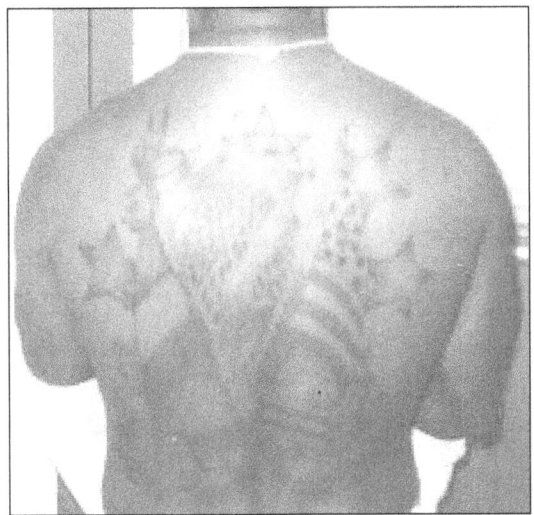

Raza Unida

The Texas Department of Criminal Justice started tracking the Raza Unida prison gang in 1991. The RU has no association with other groups that have Raza or Unida in their name. The RU is based in Corpus Christi, TX with over 300 members. Their official colors are Black and Blue. On 1/27/05, six members of the Raza Unida prison gang were arrested by agents of the ATF, FBI, Corpus Christi Police Gang Unit, Nueces County Sheriff's Dept. and Ingleside Police Dept. The arrests were the result of an Organized Crime Drug Enforcement Task Force (OCDETF) and Project Safe Streets Task Force investigation into illegal drug distribution and firearm trafficking in Corpus Christi.

The Raza Unida began to multiply in 1995 after a murderous war erupted between the TS and the Barrio Azteca. The Raza Unida refused to get involved in this war or assist the Texas Syndicate. Instead, the Raza Unida severed its alliance with the Texas Syndicate and declared complete independence. These infuriated members of the Texas Syndicate but the TS could not afford to retaliate against the RUs. While the Texas Syndicate was being consumed in warfare against their rival Barrio Azteca gang, the now independent Raza Unida was able to gain control of the prison drug trade.

Unfortunately, the Raza Unida's newfound power did not last long. In July 1997, the Texas Syndicate regained power and control of the prison system drug trade. During these war years, it became known to the TS that the RUs were importing drugs from the Brownsville, TX, and Matamoros, MX, and trafficking it to the Dallas and Houston areas, which was predominantly TS territory. In late March of 2002, RU members assaulted and killed a TS member at the Polunsky Unit, and lockdowns were ordered for all known or suspected TS and RU members and affiliates. A full scale gang war erupted between both gangs and violence erupted in units statewide as well as in cities such as Corpus Christi, San Antonio, Dallas and Houston. The Raza Unida suffered great losses and was on the verge of collapse when a conflict arose among ranking members of the Raza Unida. The RU's Dallas and southern Texas members split into two factions after the two could not reach an agreement or a truce. The majority faction is called RU Sureños, which make up members of the southern part of Texas, and the minority faction from Dallas which remains Raza Unida. The split caused a loss of morale for many of the organization's original members, and several hundred quit the gang.

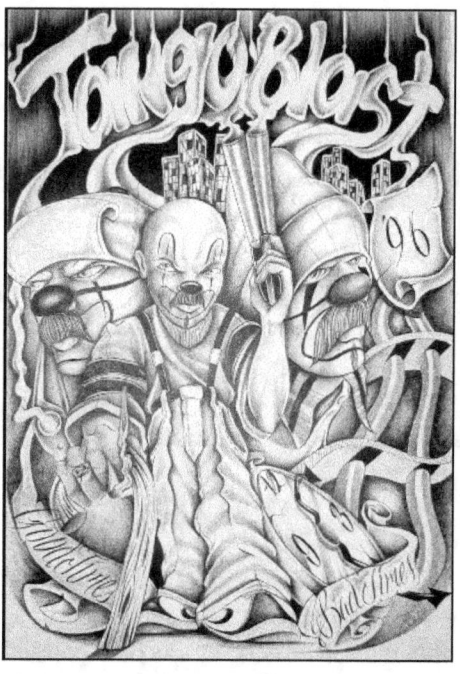

Tango Blasters

Tango Blasters or Puro Tango Blaster (PTB) were loosely organized Texas homeboy cliques that formed in TDCJ Prisons and in County Jails in the 1990s to protect themselves from other prison gangs (esquinas). In 1998, the Tango Blast prison gang is formed in the Clemens State Prison in Brazoria, Texas. They state they are not prison gangs, just groups of guys from the same neighborhoods, but as their Constitution and drawings suggest they are no different. According to Travis County Jail STG Expert Juan Garza, and TDCJ Expert Kerry Pople, they caused a lot of problems in County Jails and State Prisons.

In 2001, both the Tango Blast and Barrio Azteca engage in a gang fight in a gymnasium at the Torrez state prison in Hondo, Texas. Both gangs settle a truce soon after. On January of 2002, members of the Barrio Azteca brutally stab a Tango Blast member while the victim is using the restroom at the Robertson state prison in Abilene, Texas. A gang war between the two gangs erupts state wide soon after. On June 2002, the Tango Blast retaliates against the Barrio Azteca by severely beating 4 of its members in the John B. Connally state prison in Kenedy, Texas.

They had a full-fledged war with the Texas Syndicate. In mid-2002, the Texas Syndicate declared war on the Tango Blast prison gang, and murdered a Tango Blaster in at the J.B. Connally Unit in state prison. In June 2008, Tango Blasters attacked Texas Chicano Brotherhood members in the J.B. Connally state prison. They was also tension with the Mexikanemi due to the formation of the "Orejones" Tango Blast faction in San Antonio.

Whereas in the past, some Texas law enforcement considered the Tango Blast movement to be just a fad, they are now taken seriously. Current membership is estimated at 10,000 members. The growth of the Tangos has been fueled in part because the gang has more relaxed standards than traditional prison gangs. Tangos do not have a "blood in, blood out" philosophy where members must attack a rival to gain membership. There is no lifetime commitment. And there is no top-down paramilitary hierarchy found in gangs such as the TS or Barrio Azteca.

Tango Blast was once described by Texas authorities as being "near fad status" but it is now considered the state's biggest gang threat as it has spread to several cities, including El Paso where they were first spotted on the local radar in 2006. The Tango clique from El Paso is called "EPT" and is small compared with the much larger Barrio Azteca gang. Gang intelligence officials with the El Paso County Sheriff's Office said there are about 200 members of Tango Blast in El Paso County, with about half of them in jail, state prison or half-way houses.

Los Carnales

In the mid to late 1970's an inmate from the California prison gang called Nuestra Familia with assistance from Arnold Melon, Gilbert Gutierrez, Steve "Poyo" Baca and Felix "Animal" Martinez formed the first prison gang inside the New Mexico Department of Corrections. This group took the name Nuestra Familia and total membership of the gang was approximately 75 strong. Arnold Melon took the initial leadership role of the Organization, Gilbert Gutierrez was the Enforcer, and

Steve "Poyo" Baca was the Organization's main drug supplier. Gilbert Gutierrez then took over the leadership role from Arnold Melon. Steve "Poyo" Baca wanted the leadership role and subsequently placed a hit on Gilbert Gutierrez. The NF-Our Family thing wasn't working well.

In 1978, inmates Ricky Garcia, Sammy Mascarenas, Vincent Paul Candelaria, and Lorenzo Chavez formed Los Carnales (LC) within the New Mexico Department of Corrections. The prison gang was formed as a safety in numbers concept and to unify and protect LC members from other Hispanics inmates. Los Carnales is still predominately Hispanic with a strong support of Caucasian inmates. Although smaller in size today than the Sindicato Nuevo Mexico (SNM), Los Carnales is known to demonstrate methodical and calculating activities. The gang is split between the older generation and the younger generation in a power struggle. The younger LC are led by Robert Young and Reis Lopez and have displayed violence toward staff with the killing of a Correctional Officer. Los Carnales have been shipped out of state and are sometimes found in the BOP.4

Sindicato Nuevo Mexico

By 1973, at least two CA Mexican Mafia members were from New Mexico, George Padilla of Los Padillas, and Jose Cruz "Jimmy Joe" Lucero from Albuquerque. Both were known to have communicated back home about how the CA-EME worked to help Chicano inmates and fought against Nuestra Familia. In February 1980, the New Mexico Department of Corrections experienced the most violent prison riot in the history of the U.S. at the Santa Fe Pen. Thirty-three inmates were killed. Shortly after, the Sindicato Nuevo Mexico (SNM) officially formed. In the early 1980's, Juan Baca, Julian Romero, Billy "Wild Bill" Garcia, Marty Barros, and Richard Garcia were the leadership of SNM. Internal SNM conflicts were resolved resulting in Juan Baca being "Jefe/Don" and Jacabo Armijo was chosen as "The Godfather". Angel "Papa Smurf" Munoz also led the SNM.

Once Juan Baca took control, he ordered hits on Steve "Poyo" Baca, Felix "Animal" Martinez and Gilbert Gutierrez. Eventually, the SNM burned bridges with most prison and street gangs. A relationship with the CA-EME was tainted through problems with SUR13 connected to La EME. Conflicts for power and personal problems between some SNM members caused more problems. Gerald "Sticks" Archuleta is believed to be the most influential, most feared, and most powerful as of this date since the deaths of Juan Baca and Angel Munoz. Billy Garcia continues to have his followers; however, many members believe Garcia has lost his status in the group. Julian Romero is known to have a small number of loyal followers who rival Archuleta. When a member of the SNM is released from prison he has the obligation to meet with other SNM members in the area he relocates to, and conduct SNM business out on the streets. While out on the streets, members of SNM meet regularly to pursue criminal operations for the organization.

The Arizona Mexican Mafia

Some California EME members were from originally from Arizona or paroled back there. In the late 1970s, investigators from both states discovered the EME had members operating within the State of Arizona. It was estimated that the Old AZ EME had approximately 60 members and they copied the same style as the CA-EME. Subtle differences were tattoos of two blocked M's with a skull and bat wings above and possibly the words "Mexican Mafia" or "EME". Like the CA-EME, the Old AZ EME's prison criminal activities included: Narcotics, Extortion, Assaults, Homicides and Gambling. The Old AZ EME had alliances with the Border Brothers, Grandel, and Southside Posse, and some Sureños. The Old EME's historical enemies were previously the AZ-New Mexican Mafia.

In 1978, the Arizona Mexican Mafia split into two organizations. One kept the original philosophy and structure and currently refer to themselves as the Original Mexican Mafia, or "Califas Faction of EME". The other, which came into prominence in 1984 as the "New Mexican Mafia" of Arizona. Many assaults and murders of members of both groups have occurred as a result of each organization claiming the title of "Mexican Mafia" within the Arizona prison system with the AZ-New EME eventually outnumbering and out powering the Old EME.

Members of the New Mexican Mafia considered themselves autonomous with relation to the Original Mexican Mafia and the parent organization in California. Both groups were also aware of the growing number and power of younger SUR13 gang members within Arizona, both on the street and in prison.

In recent years, especially after New-MM were sent to the Federal BOP system, there was a truce between the Old-MM and New-MM. The new breed saw that they had little power or numbers in this new system while the Old-MM had strong allies of California EME who are very powerful in the BOP. Meanwhile, in the State of Arizona-DOC system there were not many Old-MM who were still alive. So, the peace treaty was a "win-win" situation for both sides. Per prison gang expert Frank "Paco" Marcell, currently there is no Old EME or New EME, there is only a united "Arizona Mexican Mafia". All of prison gangs, whether Black, White, or Hispanic count on bringing in new young recruits from the streets to replenish their ranks. 10

Chapter 5

STREET GANGS:

LA CLICA

Street gangs are not new, but the gang rules have changed. Older veterano members used to have a unwritten code of honor. Don't hurt women, children, or old people. Nowadays, the law is "lo más loco". The "craziest most violent" one is the most respected regardless of how many people get in the way. The Mexican Mafia did try to enforce the old rule for a while telling L.A. street gang members, "Either walk up to your enemy like a man and take care of business or face a drive-by shanking by prison knife upon sentencing to prison". But young street gang members often lack discipline. A major difference between the identification of a prison gang and a street gang is that prison gangs started in prison while street gangs formed on the street. There are far more street gang members than prison gang members, but street gang members will look up to the prison gang member as somebody who has "paid their dues". Once released from prison, many will associate with their old gang again.

Gangs are often identified by the police as "street terrorists". This identification is based on their attempts to disrupt our communities by violence and sheer terror. Some municipalities have started using street gang injunctions to bar gang members from certain areas where they congregate. These gangs advertise their control over a neighborhood by the use of graffiti, sometimes called "tags" and also called "plaqeasos". It is the newspaper of the street. Hispanic gangs have become increasingly more mobile. Interstate highways like the I-5, I-10, I-80, and I-90 corridors are used by many Latino street gang members as main routes, from south to north, west to east, for illegal activities.

Authorities estimate that Latino street gang membership numbered over 60,000 from some 450 gangs in just L.A. County alone. Many gangs both inside and outside of correctional facilities have international ties, i.e. the "18th Street Gang (XV3) and the Mara Salvatrucha (MS)". Latino gangs on the West Coast may use Mayan or Aztec symbols in art, tattoos, and sometimes in graffiti such as the Mayan number 13 or 14 or use the Aztec Nahuatl word "Kanpol" for Southern Man in the case of Sureños and "Ixpol" for Northern Man in the case of Norteños.

Florencia 13

Florencia is the second biggest Hispanic gang in L.A. and strongest in South Central Los Angeles. This area is located very close to the flashpoint of the L.A. Riots and the F13 were heavily involved in looting. The F-13 has a long running feud with the hated 18th Street gang with dozens of deaths attributed between these two major groups. Florencia and 18th Street have always been rivals but the situation got worse when the 18's started a South Side clique around the late 1980's. F13 have beefed for years with the notorious 38th St. Gang of the "Sleepy Lagoon" Case.

By the 1960s, the Florence Gang, or "Florencia" in Spanish, was respectably large in numbers and seemed to have many rivals, including Tortilla Flats, Grape Street Crips, and Hickory Street, and more recently a bloody feud with East Coast Crips (ECC). The gang's name was taken from Florence Avenue, which is a major east/west thoroughfare in South Central Los Angeles. The gang also adopted a popular song from the 1950s as their unofficial anthem. The song, Florence by the Paragons, was played at parties and events where Florencia members were present and often requested to radio disc jockeys by Florencia members as a show of disrespect to other gangs in the area. It is home for Florencia 13 and also Pancho's Bakery. In the 1960s, gangs would graffiti the walls of the bakery. An agreement was made to stop the graffiti if the owner would let them paint a mural of the Virgin of Guadalupe on the side wall of the bakery. The graffiti stopped. During the

1992 Rodney King Riots, the buildings surrounding the bakery were looted and burned. Jorge Cedillo, an owner of Pancho's Bakery, remembers, "If it hadn't been for her [the Virgin], our business would not have survived the riots. I feel it in my heart and soul.."

There are many good people living in the neighborhood. Unfortunately, there are also a lot of bad people living in this area. Today, Florencia continues to make money from drug sales and taxation of dealers and legitimate businesses in their territory in and around Huntington Park, but they have also expanded into other industries. Like several other gangs, members of Florencia have found income in document fraud, media piracy and other crimes less likely to attract law enforcement attention than illegal drug sales. 1

18th Street Gang

This gang started on the West Side of Los Angeles around 1965. It was made up largely of 2nd generation Hispanic immigrants. As the 18th Street gang began to battle with the more established Chicano gangs, they began to recruit outside of the Hispanic community. Some officials estimated their size with up to 20,000 members in over 120 U.S. cities. According to the Department of Justice, an estimated 60% were illegal immigrants. The gang became so big that most of its members did not even know each other.

The 18th Street gang also has cliques in the North Hollywood area, in East L.A. County, and in South Central Los Angeles. There are even groups of the 18th Street gang in Mexico, Guatemala, Honduras, and El Salvador, as well as other parts of the world.

According to a former Portland Gang Enforcement Team (GET) Officer, "They are now the fastest growing Hispanic gang in the State of Oregon." As law enforcement cracked down on the gang in L.A., they traveled up the West Coast to Portland, Seattle, and over to Eastern Washington.2

The following incident is an example of the Eighteenth Street gang mentality: "On June 2, 1994, as agents from the Immigration and Naturalization Service Gang Unit were driving west bound on Third Street in Downtown L.A., they approached Columbia Street. The agents recognized three individuals, one of whom they recognized as being from 18 since they had arrested him in the past.

As they stopped and exited their vehicle, the suspects ran away. One of the 18th Streeter, named "Shorty", turned and fired five shots in the agent's direction."3

From 1990 to 1996, Eighteenth Street members killed over one hundred people just in the City of Los Angeles. They taxed street venders even handing out business cards. They tagged storefronts, restaurants, and scared away customers until many owners were forced to close or pay. The gang was very involved in criminal activities during the 1992 L.A. Riots. In 1994, a combined task force of the FBI and LAPD targeted, arrested, and convicted six influential members. They've had on and off again, ties with the Mexican Mafia. Because of their close ties to the drug cartels they are a very good source of drugs for La EME. Because of their low criteria for becoming a member and lack of control due to their size, they are also perceived as a liability and they did not always follow EME orders.

Carlos "Truco" Lopez was an EME collections rep who cruised through 18th Street territory with a girlfriend in his new $35,000 Chevy Suburban. Eighteenth Street gunmen instantly lit him up with over 30 rounds of automatic gunfire. They spray-painted his vehicle with XVIII graffiti so nobody would question who did it.4

 The gang was directed by the veteranos to step up activity. The 18th Street gang was embarrassed and upset with the EME RICO trial. In addition, there were injunctions against the 18th Street Gang that were disrupting their business. In August of 1998, twenty-six year old LAPD Officer Filbert Cuesta Jr., a member of the Community Resources Against Street Hoodlums (CRASH) unit, was sitting in his patrol car when an 18th Streeter walked up towards his patrol car and shot him in the back of the head. It was a cowardly murder of a cop!

Mara Salvatrucha

The Mara Salvatrucha (MS) gang was originally made up mostly of native Salvadorans and also

originated in the West Los Angeles area. Many MS started out as being Stoners, with long hair, and into listening to "heavy metal" music. Many of them also played on soccer teams. The group was started, in part, to protect themselves from the 18th Street gang.5

Originally many officers who confronted the MS thought that "Mara" meant gang since it was used by the Maravilla gangs in East Los Angeles. "Salva" for El Salvador and "trucha" Spanish slang for beware! But as it turns out it just means Salvadoran gang. MS is also known to be very violent.

According to a Federal source, "One of the terrifying background elements of many older veterano MS members is that they may have received special forces training from the C.I.A. Others may be former guerrilla soldiers who are experts at sabotage, making bombs, creating diversions, and skilled at using weapons." However, this reputation is highly overrated and most young MS have no such training.

When deported, the MS has continued its illegal activity in El Salvador where they are extremely dangerous. In 2012, the government of El Salvador denied that they had participated in a truce arranged between 18th Street and MS gang. But the gangs bragged they could control the murder rate at will. MS have been identified in New York, Washington D.C., Oregon, Seattle, and even in Canada.

An injunction against the MS in the North Hollywood, California, proved effective. Other agencies followed suit. Police in Seattle acted swiftly to the gang. According to former SPD Gang Detective Ed Harris, "If we can deal with them at this infancy debut in Seattle in such a way that it discourages other MS gang members from coming up here, then we've gone a long way to reduce violence before it starts". His partner Detective Rod Harding specialized in "taggers" and graffiti identification. He documented, tracked the gang, took pictures of the property damage they did with their "plaqueasos", followed it up with prosecutions, deportations, and made the community aware until the MS gang decided to leave the area. Unfortunately, the MS came back in even greater numbers and to tax local gangs. You have to stay on top of MS, they are very adaptable to their environment. 6

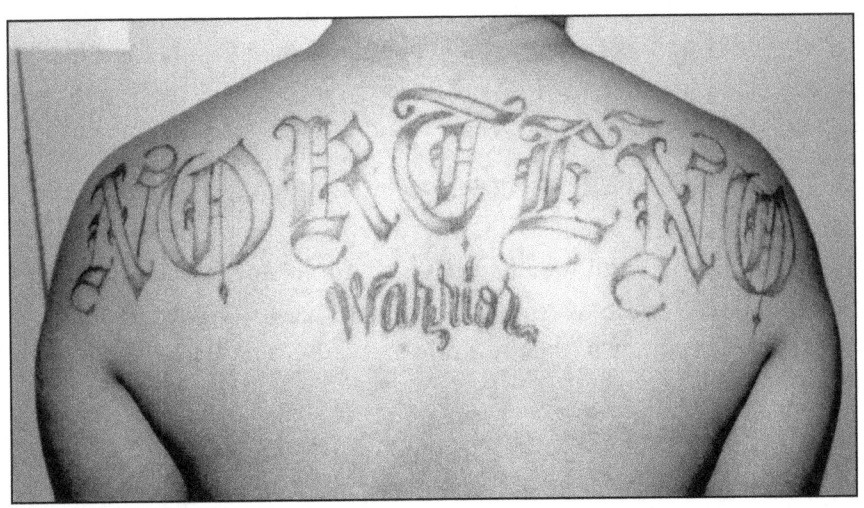

Norteños

After the Shoe War of 1968 and the death of Mexican Mafia leader "Chy" Cadena in 1972, La EME and Nuestra Familia often found their membership placed in lock down. They created young farm teams to help run their day-to-day operations similar to the relationship between Minor and

Major League Baseball. These groups became recruiting pools to groom new NF or EME members. The Southern Chicanos became known as Sureños and Northern Chicanos became known as Norteños. Northern inmates commonly used the letter "N" to symbolize their allegiance to the North, since "N" is the 14th letter (XIV) of the alphabet. The Norteños gangs also chose the color red and stole symbols from the United Farm Workers. Over the years, Norteños expanded outside of Northern California to places like Yakima, WA, but they are not as widespread across the United States as Sureños are. They claim to choose quality over quantity.

F-14 Bulldogs

The Fresno Bulldogs (F-14) have operated in Central California for well over twenty years. They took on the name of the Fresno State University Bulldogs. Their main area of activity was the East Side of Fresno. Fresno was one of the many burgeoning towns along Highway 99 in California's San Joaquin Valley. The Bulldogs had little local competition at first being the biggest gang in the area and rapidly expanded to other varrios. Later, they battled with the growing Southeast Asian gangs in the Fresno area.

When the F-14's went to prison they usually joined with the Nuestra Familia prison gang. They usually wore red and bulldog symbols with spiked collars as tattoos. In the late-1970s to mid-1980s they had a major dispute with the "Familianos" on the street over drug trafficking taxes. A major drug dealer and F-14 member was killed. This resulted in a major gang war between the NF and F-14 that reached all the way behind prison walls. The F-14 have also caused major disturbances at the Fresno County Jail. 7

The Almighty Latin King/Queen Nation

The Latin Kings grew out of the Chicago street gang wars of the 1940s and 50s. They developed a philosophy of "Kingism" and became a part of the "Peoples Nation" during the 1960s polarization of Chicago gangs. They have an established "Charter" and have well documented rules which members must strictly adhere to show "Amor de Rey". One of the biggest prisons where Latin Kings were housed was Statesville in Illinois which opened in 1925. It was a maximum security prison surrounded by a 33-foot high wall and 12 perimeter gun towers.

Entering the yard at Statesville, a young leader of the Latin Kings who was active on the street, said he knew all but two of the many Kings who were incarcerated upon his arrival. He was already connected so they hooked him up with the basic prison necessities. There were other reasons to hook up in prison.

One Latin King informant stated that an independent or non-affiliated inmate would be very hesitant to deal in large quantities of illegal goods because he could easily get caught if he accumulated too much. In contrast, a gang member had partners who could help hide or distribute the contraband. 8

During the 1970s, North and South Chicago Latin King factions developed with each choosing their own President, "Incas" or "Supreme Crown". One of their leaders, Lord "Gino" Colón, ordered a Corrections Officer to be killed in 1989 while he was in prison. Colón ruled with an iron fist. According to informant and former Inca Wilfredo "Pito" Escobar, "Everybody had to do what he said." Colón was ultimately charged with the conspiracy in 1997 along with four other members while he was housed at the Menard, Illinois, facility. He was only 24 hours away from freedom when the guilty verdict came down and he was placed back into custody.

During the 1980s, the Kings expanded and moved towards the East Coast where they became a big problem for New York City Jails, the Massachusetts Department of Corrections, and Connecticut DOC systems. There are separate factions of Kings but recently there have been efforts by the Chicago Motherland to unite them. In June of 1994, twenty members of the New York Chapter of Latin Kings and 16 in Connecticut were indicted for assault, murder, and racketeering. Luis "King Blood" Felipe was found guilty in New York in the latter part of 1996 and sent to Federal prison.

After Felipe's arrest, Anthony "King Tone" Fernandez took over for the New York Kings. He too was arrested and sent to federal prison. Under Fernandez, the Queens or female members, demanded more respect and took on an increasing role in the organization called the "Almighty Latin King/Queen Nation". However, the Chicago Motherland was against any rewriting of the Manifesto. The Kings hold meetings, sometimes called church. Their colors are gold and black often worn as religious beads.

Spanish Gangsters, Latin Disciples, Eagles, and Cobras

Groups like the Maniac Latin Disciples are historically aligned with the "Folks Nation". They usually get along with Black Gangster Disciples and other Folks groups in jail or in prison. Their hated enemies are the Latin Kings. These gang all have their own constitutions, signs, and symbols. While these groups were founded in the Chicago area, they have expanded in other areas of the Mid-West. Chicago gang expert Joe Sparks notes that the old Folks and Peoples alliances do not hold as much as they used to. As more and more gang members enter the criminal justice system, continued alliances between super-gangs will be seen nationwide. SUR13 and Norte 14 gangs are also in the Mid-West. They don't usually start wars with established gangs. They'll go in areas where the Latin Kings or Gangster Disciples aren't strong, bring in their soldiers, then intrude on areas where they think they are weak.7

More information on Mid-West Latino gangs can be found in a book by the author and Sparks called *"Chicago Gangs: Beyond Folks and People"*.

Wanna-B/Gonna-B

The term wanna-be (a gangster) has been misused so much that it is no longer used by serious gang workers. It has been used by many Mayors, Police, Adult, and Juvenile Justice Administrators to deny that they have gangs. Many times, they have ignored the problem as if it might go away like some fad.

Sometimes officials announce to the community and press that, "We don't have any real gangsters, they're just a bunch of Wanna-B's!" What they are really saying is, "We have gang members that are in their infancy". If kids want to join gangs bad enough they're going be a gangster eventually if something isn't done about it. Gangs love apathy!

While I took a tour of the Orange County, California, Juvenile Hall in the early 1990s, I heard, "I'm 18 with a Bullet" on the intercom. It is the Eighteen Street Gang's theme song. As it played the youngsters threw up the "E" and other hand signs for their gang. The message was clear, "I might be locked up but, my gang is not forgotten". These delinquent kids aren't Wanna-B's, they're Gonna-B's!

In California, the Norwalk, Chino, and Preston School for Boys were maximum housing units for offenders in the California Youth Authority (CYA). Due to some scandals the CYA was brought under the adult CDCR. The highest security juvenile facility in Washington State is Green Hill which has some good intervention programs. Unfortunately, these youthful offender institutions may be viewed by some Gonna-B's as the first stepping stone in a long illustrious criminal career. According to former Juvenile Rehabilitation Administration Gang Specialist Sherman Wilkins, "while the intent of the juvenile justice system is to rehabilitate, many kids view their treatment as a summer camp or vacation away from the streets". 9

Inside or outside of the juvenile system, junior cliques or gang clicas may form as youth become more involved in violent crime. With recent juvenile laws, there has been a huge increase in the number of youthful offenders incarcerated within the adult system that have not been previously affiliated with the gang culture and groups on the outside. These displaced youth may look to belong to a gang family.

Correctional staff should be aware that these juveniles might be prime candidates to be recruited or victimized by hardcore gang members within a facility. In addition, there may be past ties or relationships from the street to members incarcerated within the facility that remain strong. Juvenile Probation officers have extremely high caseloads and it can be very hard to track a juvenile's progress once he leaves a juvenile hall, camp, or group home. There is a lack of intervention program funding to reach all youth that truly need it. Those most likely to succeed may get little job or educational placement assistance. Youth who are at a high risk to re-offend may be the only ones really being monitored. This is a very misfortunate situation that needs to be better addressed.

In Washington State, House Bill 3900 was passed that requires juveniles suspected of violent crime be prosecuted in adult courts as automatic declines in certain situations. They are often housed with adults (unless they request protective custody) while they are fighting their cases. While many people, including myself, were concerned that these youth might be victimized, experience shows just the opposite happened. These juveniles have been so loud and reckless that even some of the adult convicts request to be separated from them. Their placement in jail has caused major headaches for adult systems. For instance, the law requires that juveniles be in school whether incarcerated or not. Many facilities were not set up to deal with this.

Recently, with calls for juvenile justice reform and changes in juvenile law, contact with the revolving door may increase causing future challenges to the Criminal Justice system, and big funding problems.

Street and prison gang members all have a story to tell. I could easily write a book on each one.

Chapter 6

The Gang Lifestyle:

Mi Vida Loca

"Jimmy Joe" was from the Old School. By his late twenties he had already been through most of New Mexico's youth and adult detention facilities, as well as New Mexico State Prison's "Hate Factory" at Santa Fe. He lived his life by the Pachuco Code, "Always walk proud like a man and never, ever, snitch!" After parole, he sought work in Los Angeles and got picked up on a robbery charge. While incarcerated at California's Folsom Prison, he was introduced to the "Carnales" (brothers) of the Mexican Mafia. Folsom was in the midst of a violent war with the Nuestra Familia gang. He earned a solid reputation and became good friends with both Joe Morgan and "Cheyenne" Cadena.

Jimmy Joe himself became suspect by prison authorities for his involvement in several stabbings and murders. When he was released from custody, he decided to travel to the city of Seattle and turn a new leaf. It didn't take long before he found a drug connection and started up his old habit again. In 1978, he was sent to the Washington State Penitentiary at Walla Walla on a burglary conviction.

When Jimmy Joe first got to "the Walls" he could only count seventy Chicano inmates, about ten who were from California. Being totally amazed and very angry to see the "Chicano Clubhouse" being run by the White "Bikers Club", JJ laid down the law that any inmate who disrespected the Chicanos would get stabbed.1

The Washington Department of Corrections (DOC) was experimenting with inmate democracy and advisory boards as a new rehabilitation method. The experiment failed miserably as the gangs virtually took over. He ended up in the Federal Bureau of Prison's Marion Facility and at the "Hothouse" in Leavenworth as punishment for conspiracy and blamed the Chicano Club's former President "Diamond" for "ratting out and talking a lot of bullshit about the brothers".

At age 58, his eyes sunken in after years of drug abuse, Jimmy Joe was again locked up for a robbery charge. He denied guilt when he was being charged on a new three-strikes law. He was admired and considered a veterano leader amongst the other Hispanic inmates. While doing a previous stint in jail, he was infracted for giving out extra food trays when he worked as a trustee. When asked to give his defense he responded, "What can I say? I'm always gonna' be a convict!"2

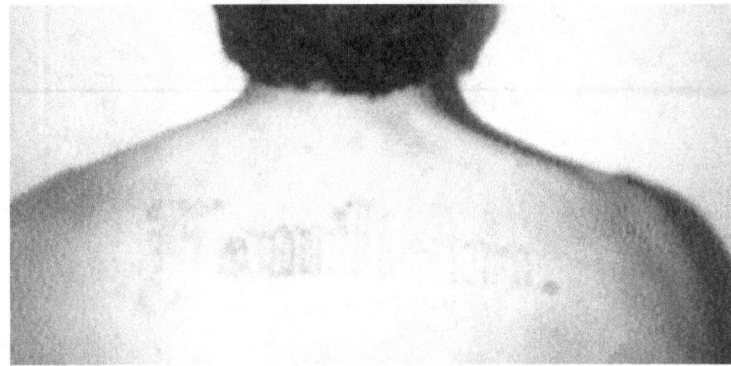

"Pancho" joined the Nuestra Familia prison gang while incarcerated at California's Deuel Vocational Institute at Tracy. "They were hitting guys right off the bus, you know, stabbing them in front of everybody. You had to clique up!" Pancho even got tattooed with the prison gang's name "Familiano" across his back. After years of surviving deadly prison wars with the hated Mexican Mafia, he decided to get out of town for not paying back a large drug debt. According to Pancho, "The Familia would have had me killed on the outs for not taking care of business". Seattle had not yet experienced the kind of gang violence that was rampant in California. Still, his heavily tattooed torso was a daily reminder of his past. He had a burning hate inside of him. "You know for a long time I couldn't look another Chicano in the eyes." Pancho was brought in to jail on a drug charge. He was very embarrassed and trying hard to kick his habit. "Man, I'm too old for this stuff…", he stated quietly.3

"Matón" was a tall cold-blooded killer who had a long hard empty stare. After he did time in 1977 for killing a guy in Texas who "screwed him" over, he came up north to Washington State. He became a member of the Texas Syndicate in 1980 when he was courted in by another Tejano while he did time at the Federal Detention Center-El Reno. When he was released, he soon did time on another case at the Idaho State Pen so he was quite institutionalized. Matón was a huge disciplinary problem and was being held in the Intensive Management Unit (IMU). Matón was put on a behavior management plan to get him to comply better with the rules and regulations of the facility. "I've had a chiva habit (heroin) for a long time ése", he whispered somberly. Then he yelled out loud so the other inmates could hear, "and fuck those Mafia putos, everybody knows, you don't mess with Texas!"4

"Lil' Moreno" was from the varrio of Primera Flats in East Los Angeles. He was doing time on an auto theft conviction and placed on probation and in a Azusa, California, group home. Moreno had already did time at Los Padrinos Juvenile Hall and was about to be put in the California Youth Authority (CYA) when he found a bed at the Boy's home. "Man this place ain't shit! Nothing but busters up in here! I got to get up out of here Homes!", he said to another resident. Moreno had been born in the varrio and felt "violence solves everything". At least that was what the big Homies said. He had an older brother in the adult system at the Corcoran Security Housing Unit of the California Department of Corrections.

Moreno had dreams of making it to the big time himself. He already had one "Absence Without Leave" and had been caught getting high after school several times. He left the group home and was sent to the YA after he was captured, and he was happy as he was well on his way to the "Big House".5

"Big Al" grew up in a gang, he didn't join one. His father used to be associated with the Mexican Mafia. In order to get away from the California gang scene, he brought his family to Washington. In spite of his father's wishes Al respected the older cholo gangsters. "'P', 'Silent', 'Lalo', 'J' and me started the South Side Locos. Before us there was the CIA, Chicanos in Action, and the Vatos Locos, but basically we started that gang bang shit up here in Seattle." Concerning his recent arrest Al commented, "Those UL fools tried to jump my brother. Man, they already jumped him once. (His brother was later killed.) I pulled out all my shit in the trunk and blasted them and they all scattered! Then the damn police took away my guns!" Big Al just couldn't understand why the police would want to take away his weapons.6

"Penguin" was one of the "Original Gangsters" of the "United Latino" (UL) gang. His friends called him Penguin because of the way he walked and talked. As a teenager, he began drinking, smoking weed, and stealing cars around the Northgate area when school got too boring. All of his homeboys were from similar backgrounds of poor working class families. "You know I've tried to do good and straighten out, but I just can't seem to make the right moves", he said. "Those pínche 13's are always talking their shit and messing with us, then I got to back up my Homies." Penguin was praised by social workers for being a bright but delinquent youth. He liked to read and draw about Chicano and Latino culture of the past. For now, all Penguin could do is worry about the present, try to hold down his part time job, his dream of being a movie producer, and stay out of trouble.7

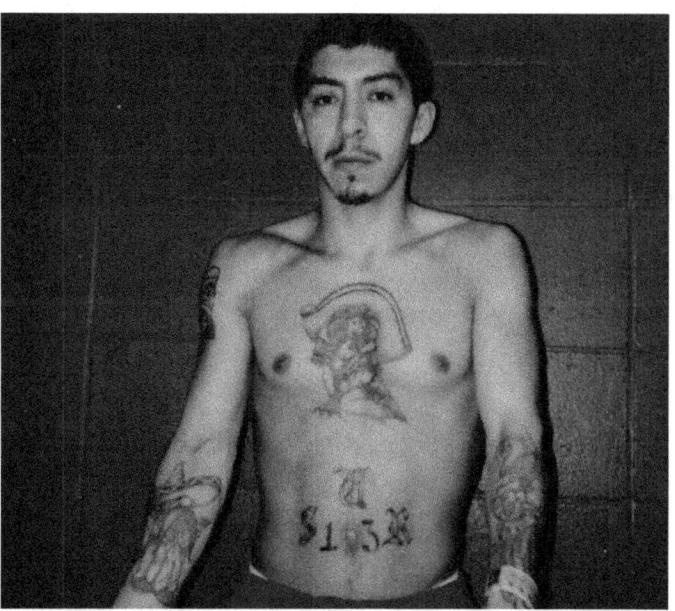

"Sadboy" was a small but rugged kid. His older brother was a hardcore member of a San Jose Norteño 14 gang and was locked up at San Quentin. Sadboy was affiliated with the Varrio Locos and had SUR 13 tattooed across his whole stomach. He mostly did car prowls and petty thefts but had no major criminal record until he made a drug deal with some acquaintances. "These guys pulled up to sell some mota, some weed, but I saw they had a gun. I thought they were going to rob me so I shot them with my piece." Although he seemed remorseful, he had few real expectations of what was to follow. He was now looking at seven years in prison for a tragic and foolish mistake.8

"Mousie" was born in the rural town of Sunnyside, Washington. In 1974, her family moved to the Roxbury Village Projects in West Seattle. She was half-Puerto Rican and half-Mexican. Mousie's dad was a heroin addict, while her mother was a stoned alcoholic. She remembers, "There was a lot of fighting and yelling, even at late hours of the night. It was hard to study for school with all of the noise."

At fifteen years old, she ran away from home when she got pregnant by her boyfriend. Mousie's older sister turned tricks for extra money and became a victim of the "Green River Killer" serial murders. Her dad and older brother both overdosed and died of heroin. One of her brothers became heavily involved in gang banging, while another was having a domestic violence problem with his wife. Mousie had few marketable job skills and became very desperate. Her husband had kicked her out of their house and was smoking crack, so she pulled a robbery job in an effort to help support and feed her kids. To top it all off, her oldest child was raped after she was arrested (She was later killed in a quadruple homicide).

Her husband only called her "a bitch and a hole" during her trial instead of coming to her defense. Mousie was at least glad to find a responsible relative to get custody of the kids when she went to prison at the Washington Correctional Center for Women.9

"Huero" was a member of the Latin Kings. He became affiliated with the Kings while working as a hustler on the mean streets of Chicago. He did several stints at the Cook County Jail before he got sent off to Joliet prison on a burglary charge. This was the same prison depicted in the movie "Blues Brothers". He stated, "I got out and paroled to Cicero and started right back hanging out with my Peeps."

Soon he got shipped off to Menard on a robbery conviction. "I wanted to start a new life you know, but it's hard and all these cops are assholes." He had a rough time finding anyone who would hire him given his record, so he started fencing and forging checks. Huero soon winded right back up in the system he grew up and felt most comfortable in.10

"Champ" was a member of the Tortilla Flats Gang from Compton located just south of South Central L.A. "I got caught up in a bad situation and caught a life sentence for murder just to back up the 'hood. Champ got accustomed to doing time after an initial period of depression. He kept busy by refereeing inmate sports events at Folsom Prison and was well liked by staff for his demeanor. Unfortunately, some hardcore Sureños did not like his friendship with Black inmates and talk about penitentiary politics so they "stuck him" on the yard. He pondered over the reason why violence was so prevalent amongst poor people from the same neighborhoods who really had nothing to fight over.11

"Coneja" was born to a large Mexican family who came from the Santa Clara Valley. She had a son when she was very young, but her old man left her. Her family moved to the Yakima Valley where she became a big sister to Chicana gang members with Norteño affiliations. "I'd smoke a little mota, tu sabes, and cruise my green Chevy Impala to check out the fine guys and naturally recruit some of the homegirls into la clica." Coneja would deal dope for her brothers and became pretty good at it until she got "popped". She asked, "Tell me, what else can I do to make that kind of money?"12

"Chato" was from Pico Rivera, California, located just East of East Los Angeles. When he was very young he witnessed his brother get executed on orders of the Mexican Mafia. His brother had violated gang rules. Still, this did not stop Chato from entering the gangster lifestyle. He soon joined a gang called Vatos Locos 13. When asked if he'd ever leave the gang, he shrugged. "I don't know, it's hard, once you get in seems like you can't get out?" His gang's favorite pastime besides drinking and drugging was stealing cars. Chato got to be very good at it. Finally, his night shift on the streets caught up to him and he was sent to prison. When asked how he felt about it, "Man, I'm lucky cause most the OG's I know got deported to Mexico, so it looks like I'm OG now!" 13

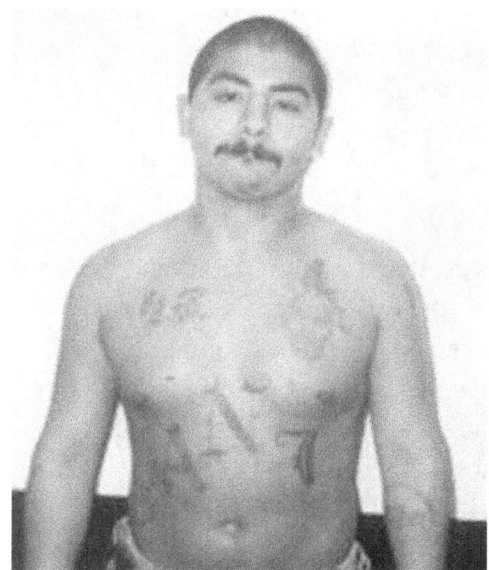

"Moke" was a Norteño from the Las Palmas 14 gang. He was born in Seattle, but when his parents got a divorce he went to live with his dad in San Jose, California. He was considered a martial arts expert like his dad and learned how to fight at an early age. When he was in the Karate Dojo he was well disciplined, but out on the streets he ran wild. He soon found himself on the Big Yard at San Quentin for a firearms conviction. He walked the same ground as Nuestra Familia gang members did decades before him. While at SQ he was recruited into the Northern Structure and got tattooed. His own brothers and sister ran with the Sureños 13 gang which caused some problems. "We couldn't be on the same yards on them inside, it's a green light on each other, if I talked to them I'd suffer the repercussions with all the other Norteños", he said reflectively. Yet, while he respected his homeboys and still liked to where San Francisco 49'ers gear, he still loved his family, "Really, they all I got!" 14

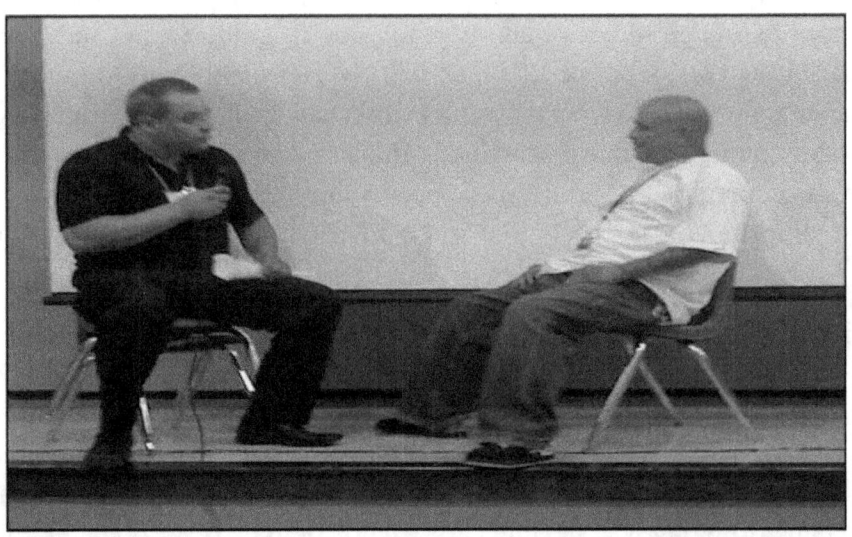

"Buzz" was born in Billings, Montana, but claimed Varrio East Side Los (VES-LOS) clique when he moved to East Los Angeles at the age of 4. He grew up in the middle of multiple warring gangs like Varrio Nueva Estrada, White Fence, Primera Flats, Hazard, and Maravilla. When he was a young teen, the older homies sent him to check out a rival gang member they gunned down to make sure he was really dead. It was no big deal for him, seeing people killed in his neighborhood was a common occurrence. His brother Puppet was from the same varrio and was killed in gang violence at the ripe age of twenty years old. In 1986, Buzz was convicted of a robbery and sent to the Reception Center at Vacaville. It was at Vacaville that he earned his Camarada stripes and became a Rep for the Sureños by reporting directly to the Mexican Mafia.

When released he picked up a really bad heroin habit and did several more stints locked up. He joined a lowrider club and loved to cruise the calles (streets), but a low point in his life came when his son from Azusa 13 was locked up and was starting to live a life of crime just like he had. Buzz didn't like what he saw and decided he better start being a better father and role model. He also started mentoring youth in a gang violence prevention program. Who better than he to rap to young people and teach them about the dangers of living "La Vida Loca", the crazy life? 15

Chapter 7

Chicano/Latino Music and Gangster Rap

There has been a lot of media coverage in the past concerning Black East Coast-West Coast Gangster Rappers, especially after several high-profile gang related cases dealing with these individuals, groups, and companies. Time-Warner that took this into consideration when Ice-T put out violent songs on his CD "Body Count". It severed his contract. Ice-T tried to make it a debate over censorship, cops had a problem with the glorification of violence on songs like "Cop Killer".

There are also gang influences with some Latino music groups. It is important to know that "Oldies and Rap" are very popular with the "Homies" or gang-bangers of today. This influence goes all of the way back to the Pachuco days with songs that were made after the 1940's Zoot-Suit Riots of in L.A. and other big cities. The "Pachuko Hop" was made by Chuck Higgins who grew up in Aliso Village barrio. On the success of that song another release was made by Higgins called the "Wetback Hop". No doubt, this would cause quite a controversy today.

A man named "Chico" Sesma promoted L.A. area concerts and had a popular radio program with Chicano youth in the 1950s, some of them gang members. "In particular Chicanos loved ballads sung by Black artists, the so-called Doo Wop groups." Ricardo Valenzuela from Pacoima, better known as Ritchie Valens, was just one of the many popular Latino singers in Southern California who played at concerts in El Monte's Legion Stadium, Pomona Auditorium, and other music halls. DJ Art Leboe recorded many of these songs on his "Oldies, but Goodies" compilations. Another popular DJ during this time period was Dick Hugg, better known as "Huggy Boy". Today gang members listen to similar radio shows that air such as "The Sancho Show" in southern California and the "Bajito Onda Show" in northern California.

The song "Louie, Louie", still a popular favorite at Mexican-American weddings, was the subject of an FBI investigation (one of Edgar J. Hoover's many paranoid delusions). It was almost banned by rightwing politicians because of its mix of white, black, and Chicano music. A Seattle based band called the Kingsmen made it very popular amongst 1960s youth. The 1960s and early 1970s brought songs and lyrics by East. L.A. bands like Thee Midnighters who wrote a song called

"Whittier Boulevard" (a famous lowrider cruising strip) who culminated their career with the East L.A. Riot song of "Chicano Power". It was very popular amongst members of the "Brown Berets" and Chicano gang members sometimes called "Batos Locos" according to Chicano music historian David Reyes.

A band called El Chicano made famous a Latin jazz tune called Viva Tirado (which roughly translates to "long live throwing down," a reference to getting into the party groove and for a Bullfighter named Jose Tirado). The term "throwing down" is now a reference to throwing gang hand signs in today's street gang culture. This song was later sampled by Kid Frost in his song, "This is for La Raza", which was heavily ganginfluenced. The video for the song prominently depicts many Cholo-style gangsters.

There are other songs that are gang influenced or have been adopted by gangs as their theme songs. "I'm Eighteen with a Bullet" is the 18th Street Gang's theme song. "Slippin' into Darkness" by WAR is popular amongst tecatos/junkies. "Natural High" by Bloodstone was very popular amongst Pirus in prison. While these songs are also listened to by non-gang members, there are some music groups who are increasingly involved in hardcore promotion of gang warfare and violence towards cops (and corrections). Some of the Latino gangsta' rappers make Kid Frost's "La Raza" look like a church hymn.

Over the years I've heard many people talking and wondering about "Smile Now, Cry Later" or Happy Face/Sad Face tattoos on gang members. It all started from a 1960's song by "Sonny (Ozuna) and the Sunliners" called "Smile Now, Cry Later" which appeared as a repro on the "East Side Story" lowrider records (now in reprint) that were popular in the seventies. From my dealings with Chicano gang members, it signifies "Mi Vida Loca". Running the streets and partying with my friends and "Homies", then when I get busted, put in jail or prison and away from my loved ones, end up crying later. "Los Solidos" gang from Connecticut also use this symbol and I have seen it on non-Chicano gang members.

Be careful with this, according to Al Valdez formerly with the Orange County DA's Office, "The smile now cry later, has to do with the craziness of gang life. Play now and pay later. It is a generic gang tattoo, not gang specific, having it alone might not make the wearer a gangster by court standards."[1]

Retired L.A. Sheriff's Sgt. and EME expert Richard Valdemar adds, "There are many, once popular, songs associated with street gangs in Los Angeles. In the 1950s, "Florence" by the "Paragons" was adopted by both Florencia 13, (the second largest street gang in Los Angeles) and the "Lynwood Paragons." In the 1960s, the Little Valley gang of East Los Angeles sang; "bad is bad and sad is sad, but you mess with Little Valley and that's too bad!" from "Little Valley" on the flip side of a classic oldie. In the 70s and 80s, even the Big Homies got into the act. The Mexican Mafia Prison gang's theme song by El Chicano became "Sabor A Me" and the Nuestra Familia's Corrido was "La Mensaje de la Nuestra Familia".

Today, Los Angeles gang members can be heard playing and singing (the Chicano style of) Black Gangsta' Rap known locally as "legal dope". Not only is there Norteño and Sureño rap, but recently Southern gang members who are opposed to the Mexican Mafia (Green Lighters) have been singing their version of a popular rap song; "Green-Lighters, Green-Lighters, Green-Lighter Riders!" This was done in defiance of the Sureños incarcerated nearby in the L.A. county jail gang modules.

Ret. Sgt. Ron Stallworth of the Utah Dept. of Public Safety wrote several books on the subject of gangster rap and even testified at a capital homicide trial in Texas in which rap lyrics were the subject of the case in point. Law Enforcement around the country has become more and more concerned each year with the rap industry's growing influence on gangs and crime. Det. Wayne Caffey of LAPD has also documented gang ties to many of these gangster rap groups.

Rap is part of the Hip-Hop culture that started on the East Coast in the mid-seventies with such groups as the Sugarhill Gang, Curtis Blow, and Grandmaster Flash. It is a diverse music style and one subgroup could be classified as "Gangster Rappers". Chicano/Latino MC's may rap in English, Spanish, or Nahuatl, or whatever. Increasingly, non-Latino artists are mixing Spanish lyrics in their music in an effort to reach out to the growing Latino market.

As far as the East Coast, it is still mostly Black rappers on the scene with some who have ties to the Crips and quite a few with ties to Blood gangs. A Puerto Rican rapper out of New York City, Big Pun, signed on with major label BMG. His big megahit single, "I'm Not A Player," made him one of the top solo Latino rappers. He sold over 1.3 million units and was the first solo Latino rapper to go platinum. When he died, he was made out to be a rap hero, but he also had "Cop Killer" lyrics.

This is the rap that got Big Pun(isher) his first break to record with the popular rapper Fat Joe. It is what they call "spittin' into the mike with dope rhymes":

"Yo, I cause a bloody bath

to make my buddies laugh

and gig my nutty wrath

I'll live as long as I'm a nasty kid

<I blast a pig and slit his throat>

just for Toom and El (Ed. Payback on the cops)

My skills are human still

Joker puffin' boom in hell

I doom the world like I was God

and <throw my gun away>

Then snatch the moon out the sky

and blow the sun away

Me and my brothers play hardball

Strictly <hardcore> lyrics

'til I'm finished breakin' God's laws

My job's raw, but I gotta' do it

I'm feelin' high then buddahead

So you <might get shot and lose a lot of fluid>

The spot, I blew it, at an early age

ever since the curly braid

I would earn a wage <with a 30 gauge>

There's <dirty ways to get paid>

if you got the balls just <load the Glock>

and cause <the hardest cop to drop his drawers>

Don't stop or pause let the shotty go up his butt (Shoot cops)

To finish up, punchin' body blows and upper cuts!"

It might be very easy for the reader to conclude that much of this ethnic music is gang-related. That is definitely not the case. Oldies are popular with the general public and many criminal justice workers too. Rap can be a healthy way for youth to express themselves given positive lyrics as shown by rappers like Robert "Battleax" Ornelas.

The gang lifestyle has influenced songs of many Latino singers and bands that grew up in gang infested neighborhoods. This music in turn may influence the behavior of the younger gang member/listener but is not necessarily indicative of gang involvement. Corrections and Law Enforcement should just be aware of the culture and the gang members' attune for music which could be a door-opener in an interrogation or interview to connect and relate with an inmate or suspect. The growing violence in the lyrics of these songs is something to be concerned about for officer safety and security of all of our communities. 2

Other than a few very early articles on the Chicano/Latino Rap evolution in underground media sources, I was the first person to public ally and critically analyze Chicano/Latino rap and its role in violence among young people. I was preceded by many knowledgeable sources on the national Black rap scene before Latino rappers "blew up". I have been accompanied in recent years by credible gang experts like Ernest Cuthbertson and Edwin Santana.

My own interest in the subject began in the late 1970s when the Hip-Hop craze spread from New York City to other areas of the United States and out to the West Coast. Hip Hop was devised by young artists in the "Big Apple" as an alternative to street gang culture and was also supported by many people in the community including Probation Officers and Gang Intervention Workers.

They tried to prevent the "Gangs of New York" violence that had been going on for 150 years. Hip Hop culture washed away many Latino and Black street gangs like Savage Nomads, Dirty Dogs, and Black Skulls. Within this movement evolved one of four elements known as "Rap". Rhyming to sample beats was a reflection of the streets without violence. Per 206 Zulu's King Khazm, "Conflict was solved through MC battles."

I was a part of the Disco Era in Seattle, WA, and remember hearing Sugar Hill Gang's "Rapper's Delight", Curtis Blow's "The Breaks", Grand Master Flash and the Furious Five's "The Message" in the early 1980s in my hometown of Yakima. I first became familiar with "Kid Frost" and his Spanglish lyrics on a demo tape from a Marine Corps buddy who was in "Black Tie Productions" and played at events in the L.A. area where Frost also first performed around 1984. My uncle was, and is still, in a well-known Latino band in the L.A. area.

I was familiar with members of the Seattle Emerald City Breakers. Later, I saw a few Hip-Hop movies come out like "Beat Street" and "Breakin'" where the "B-Boys" did not look or dress very "gangster". They were "B" movies that were almost laughable were it not for the music soundtrack, the latter which included a relatively new L.A. rapper named "Ice-T" on the cut "Reckless".

I was also familiar with many graffiti artists from New York to Seattle. In addition, I knew several MCs and DJs like Nestor "Nasty Nes" Rodriguez who worked with "Sir Mix-a-Lot" and Easy-E.

Over the years, I've met individuals with 6th grade educations who are very intelligent in street knowledge and life in general. You can have a Doctor's Degree and still have no common sense, morality, or any good sense in family values. Pancho McFarland is an Assistant Professor of Sociology at Chicago State University who wrote a book in 2008 called "Chicano Rap; Gender and Violence in the Post-Industrial Barrio". McFarland is a self-proclaimed Chicano Nationalist.

He states gang violence has decreased, actually it is the murder rate that has decreased in recent years. Just look at 50 Cent, shot nine times and still lives! Medical Trauma Centers around the nation take the credit for much of this. If paramedics get there in time, they can keep just about anybody alive. While overall crime has decreased in most U.S. cities, gang crime is still very high.

But I ask if in fact crime has gone down, then why has the use of violence in rap lyrics gone up? If rap just reflects violence in society, isn't this an exaggeration of real life in tha' Hood? McFarland says he studied 470 Chicano/Latino rap songs and over 70% of them contained violence. Much of gangster rap is also materialistic and sexist. Very few of these songs talk about how to be a good father figure or husband. Perhaps that is just ok behavior to display as claimed by gang and music experts like Professor McFarland?

Unfortunately, some young Chicanos today believe they have to look/act gangster to show they're proud of their culture and say they don't want to be a punk/nobody's fool. To some gang and non-gang members, all Cops are Bad, they say all Cops discriminate and brutalize people. This is a grossly exaggerated stereotype. Wouldn't this be like some Cops saying, all Mexicans are Bad? The fact is, as I covered in *"Ending Black and Brown Violence in America"*, a few people act bad in all professions and in all communities.

Recently, there has been a growing movement by "Hardcore Gangsta' Rappers" against "Studio Gangsters". Often these are real gangsters with little to no vocal skills, and sometimes poor lyrical skills, that dis(respect) rappers who talk about the gangster lifestyle but haven't really lived it. Charlie Row and Hi-Power Soldiers are an example of this. Increasingly, there has also been racial conflict embedded in songs. This may be in part due to a reflection or perceived tension of Black vs. Brown problems in Los Angeles, shown intensely in California prisons as pushed by the Mexican Mafia's agenda. Chino Grande even calls out Snoop Dogg on YouTube for making the song "Vato" with Cypress Hill rapper B-Real. He says, "Snoop, you ain't no motherf---ing vato!", while he and his homeboy are sitting on a couch mean mugging. Towards the end of his drib he takes off his shirt to show his muscles and numerous gang tattoos in a menacing manner. Some so-called artists may take it further, go out and commit violence in order to get that "Street Cred".

In spite of people like McFarland who make excuses that violent rap is just a harmless vent for poor male Chicanos in barrios (they'd likely be considered upper middle class in many other poor countries), it has been proven by past example that some youth will act out on violent lyrics they hear. For example, Andreas Raya, was an AWOL Marine who never saw combat in Iraq, yet he went on a personal mission in Ceres, CA, to gun down cops. His own family was obviously in denial, but in his locker were numerous items and photos showing association with Norteños 14 gangs. Also, in his personal property was a book by now pastor and x-gang member Sir Dyno of "Dark Room Familia" called "Midst of My Confusion".

DRF is the same rap company that made the song, "Die You Fu--ing Pig" with lyrics like "I wanna' hear my motherf---ing Glock go pop!" and repeated chorus line, "Die You Fu--ing Pig!". Police later found a CD player in the poncho Raya wore the night he killed Ceres PD Sgt. Howard Stevenson and gunned down other Officers. The player held a gangster rap CD titled "Season of Da' Siccness" and it is dominated by lyrics about killing people.

In an ironic twist, Robert "Huero" Gratton, the producer and promoter of Dyno's work on the Generation of United Norteños (G.U.N.) CD was killed in a car accident on Hwy 14 in July, 2008, in Palmdale, CA, located in Southern California. The self-professed NF Captain Gratton was allegedly backed up by the Nuestra Familia prison gang which advocated doing something about their "frustration of the Skrapa Invasion" or broken down as Sureños encroaching on Norteño territory. Gratton later turned police informant. Another key figure who marketed Norteño rap, Ryan "Woodie" Wood committed suicide in 2007.

There are newer rap styles that come out as the movement evolves. Some Latino Rappers have been a part of these trends like Latin Thizz by Julio "Gold Toes" Sanchez. A rapper named Jose "Conejo" Martin belonged to a L.A. gang called Harpys. Wanted for murders, he extols his criminal life on the run, and makes personal analogies to Al Capone. He raps with Texas rapper Capone, not to be confused with San Gabriel Valley rapper Capone-E.

The gangster rapper, "Cuete" (Spanish slang for a "Gun", and not the same individual as another rapper called "Lil Cuete"), hails from Redondo Beach, CA, and was in a gang called North Side Redondo (NSR). He has no real criminal record but advocates for violence against law enforcement. On his 2008 release "Heat Under The Seat", 8th Track, is a song called "Death On

A C.O." It is very disturbing due to making reference to killing a Correctional Officer. Violence on Police Officers has gone up and I think it is safe to say that songs like this have a role in it and that is no little exaggeration. This is not having an understanding of violence in society, but garbage that can infect minds of unstable individuals. People like McFarland make excuses and justify these lyrics as a way to fight against police repression.

Some groups, like the appropriately named Psycho Realm, promote open war against the State rather than work hard to improve the system. Others like Midget Loco encourage guys to "rep their hood" and "keep it gangsta". People often get shot during or after. Of course, not all Chicano/Latino rappers are Gangster Rappers. I've listened to a variety of material from all music styles. Some is not violent, many have catchy samples, complex and intelligent lyrics, and can even teach young people a thing or two about life.

Daddy Yankee mixed Spanish and English lyrics with a Reggaeton beat and became very successful and crossed over on charts. Artists like Columbian Shakira mix songs with Haitian rapper Wyclef Jean who was with the Fugees. One of my favorite artists of all time, spiritual Carlos Santana, used Wyclef raps and talent. MTV Tr3s videos use Spanish and English showcasing many Latino Rappers. 3

Today there are Asian rappers, Native American rappers, and Whites who also rap. Of course, gangster rap is not the cause of all violence in the U.S., but it plays a part. Violence has and will go up and down over the years due to a variety of social, economic, and environmental factors.

The focus of my rap articles and books; *"Varrio Warfare"* and *"Prison Gangs in America"*; however, was to show violence in lyrics and talk about violence on the street and in prison. I do not feel these types of songs do much to help young Raza, but will help get more killed and incarcerated.

I was born in the barrio and raised in and near the Projects. I've fought against gang violence most of my life. I played a trumpet in my youth and was in Seattle's All-City Band. I've helped kids do colorful murals in barrios and community centers. I've written and taught youth how to write poetry. I karaoke now and then and often people are amazed I can actually sing. For a sample see my song on YouTube "Thank God!"

I've done community work in California and across the nation to combat violence. I'll keep monitoring rappers out there and will continue to expose those who advocate violence. Several of the gangster rappers I've talked about even threatened me with legal action or insinuated that I might end up hurt. In the end, I think I must've worried them that I might hurt their standings with young people or decrease sales they tried build up based on their gangster image. If you are a positive rapper and really interested in helping the culture of Hip Hop and making your community, this world, a better place for families to live in, then I commend you for your hard work and studio skills. 4

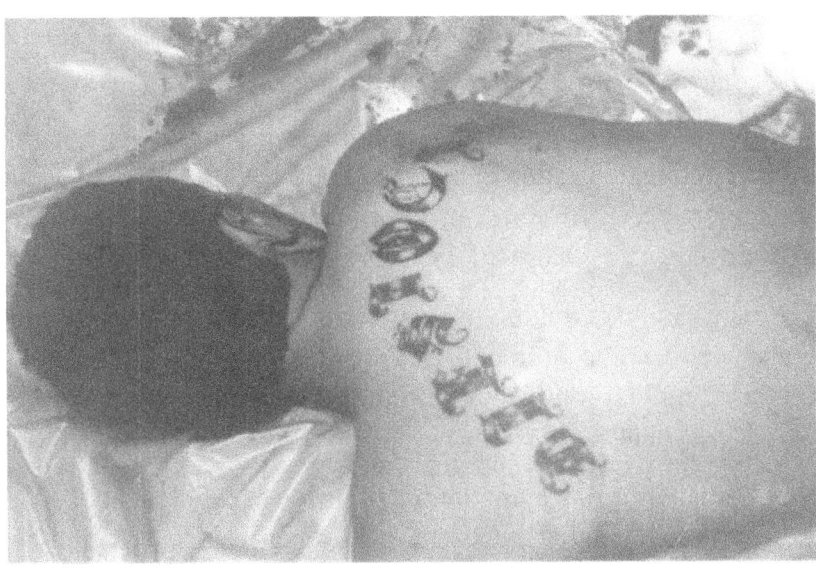

Chapter 8

VARRIO WARFARE

Whether exaggerated in song or lived in real life, there is a direct correlation between gangs, drugs, guns, and violence. Many people argue that we often treat the symptoms of gang violence in America but not the root causes and I agree. Some people even argue that delinquent behavior is a just response to the institutionalized violence of the society in which they live. They claim that in some urban centers, such as East Los Angeles, Latino gang members consist of as much as 40% of the population. I am not so sure that is true, but some psychosocial theorists such as Erik Erikson argues that such a gang identity is a healthy part of growing up.

Identity formation or "Ego" is the process through which an adolescent defines his or her own roles, values, beliefs, and goals. Youth find themselves in a state of social instability characterized by an unstructured social and psychological reality. It is during this period of instability that a youth can experience a desperate need for social bonding which is often met through the formation of a peer group, a clique, or gang.

As gang members become more and more caught up in the gangster lifestyle they disconnect more and more from other areas of their life. They start "associating" with gang members. Members tell them that if they are proud of their race then they will clique up with their peers. Once recruits are accepted into the group through courting in and a process of gang rituals such as "jump-ins", their gang member identity becomes more and more intense. Pretty soon, the kid who grew up as the individual named Juan, now becomes the alter ego of "Capone" or "Mad Dog" or "Trigger". They then often live up to that name and reputation for violence. The gang member is told by the clica that he must fight other gangsters to prove himself and so that their varrio will not be seen by others as being weak. Females are also told they have to fight other girls "if they are down". As

the member spends more and more time in the gang, he or she creates enemies, then often feel the urge they have to stay in the gang for protection. Rivals are made out to be sub-human via name calling and other signs of disrespect. Peers reward them for this slander by pumping up their egos as being modern day warriors.

Probably the biggest factor that I have seen amongst incarcerated youth is the lack of schooling. Many say they completed their education on average up to the 10th grade, meaning they dropped out during their sophomore year. However, many of them can only read or write at the 3rd or 4th grade level. Some of them cannot even spell their own names let alone fill out a job application.

At the same time many Latino youth face the challenge of cultural assimilation and peer acceptance. They also are trying to fit in and make progress in school. When they fail, the gang moves in to recruit them, and tells them they would be a great gang member. After a few pats on the back and atta-boys the youngster feels success, at least at something, even if it is bad.

The same goes for females, but playing hooky during or after school often has different consequences for them. We all know that teens going through puberty have raging hormones, but include drugs and alcohol in the mix, and their inhibitions are lowered even more. Statistics show that the highest crime and pregnancy rates among Latinas are between the hours of 4 and 6 pm, when students leave school and have little supervision. Many of these young mothers' own mothers were very young when they had them so they may not have good parenting skills.

Gang culture thrives on boredom and finds exciting things for idle kids to do. Lack of recognition in school leads to high recognition on the streets, lack of recreational alternatives often leads to gang banging as a sport.

The Hispanic gangs of the Pachuco and Vato Loco era were largely into alcohol, marijuana, and occasional heroin use when they got older. During the 1970s, some Hispanic kids started forming "Stoner" groups. They listened to heavy metal music, got high, and sometimes tagged areas with graffiti just like traditional Hispanic gangs. The use of a strong tranquilizer known as Phencyclidine (PCP) was seen during the late 1970s. The drug got its street name after a popular brand of thin brown cigarettes called "Shermans" (Sherms) were dipped in the toxic chemical of "Angel Dust". Street gang members really liked the feeling of invincibility it gave them during a fight. PCP also had lots of side effects and a bad reputation.

While the whole country was experiencing the "Cocaine Epidemic" in the 1980s, it was widely known to DEA authorities that the Colombians and other Latin American drug cartels were funneling in enormous quantities of "coca" into the U.S., many times through the Miami area. When there was a crackdown in the Gulf, smugglers started to transport it across the Mexican border as described in Chapter 3 and in my book *How We Lost the Drug War*.

But, Latino drug cartels were not the only ones importing drugs to America. The L.A. Crips and Bloods got "Crack Cocaine" trafficking down to a science. Both Gangster Disciples and Vice Lords were known to deal enormous quantities of drugs in the Midwest. Some Hispanic gangs also later began to deal the smokeable form of cocaine called "Crack", whereas previously they usually dealt in heroin or marijuana. Many experts say the evolution of street gangs to provide drugs was a major step towards organized crime.[1]

The surge in drug usage was like a cancer across America. According to former U.S. Drug Policy Chief, General Barry McCaffery, "Community action against drug problems must be the heart of the solution. There is no national drug problem, but a series of epidemics." General McCaffery stated that the United States has over 12 million drug users and 6 million addicts who consume over 50 billion dollars in drug consumption each year.

Approximately 40 billion of that amount goes to Mexican Drug Cartel networks today. Even small towns, like my place of birth, were affected by the drug epidemic. In 1994, the City of Yakima, located in Eastern Washington was voted an "All-American City". People in law enforcement and Hispanic community also called it the "gang capitol of the state". It was a vivid example of the growth of gangs, drugs, and weapons.

It's been my experience that many drug dealers don't belong to a gang and operate as independents; however, often they will associate and do business with gang members. They tell me, "Morales, I'm not a banger, I'm a slanger!" In other words, they are not jumped into a gang, but sell dope and will do business with gangs if need be. Many people will use drugs for recreational purposes and deal a little on the side to support their habit.

Most of these drugs are extremely addicting. Some break the cardinal rule of dealing, "never became your own best customer". They will stoop so low as to rip their own families off. The downward spiral continues until they need more money and start doing burglaries. They became more desperate for a fix, do robberies, and eventually end up in jail. They often clean up in custody, but once released, return to old habits.

As drug consumption rose steadily each year throughout the 1990s, other street drugs became more common. Methamphetamine was first known as a "Biker's drug" since many of the Outlaw Motorcycle Gangs produced it. Many of the ingredients to make "Meth" could be found at your local Ace Hardware Store. Users stated they could stay up for days on the stuff. Meth users could easily be misidentified as mentally ill as they will display behavior known as "tweeking", uncontrollable movements and twitching of the body. One of the main ingredients is ephedrine and the other chemicals used in the production of this drug are extremely hazardous and toxic. When the DEA and other agencies began to crack down on "Crystal Meth" in the U.S., Mexican gangs stepped in to supply the rapidly growing demand of "crank" users. Methamphetamine seizures at the U.S.-Mexican border rose from 6.5 kilograms in 1992 to 665 kilograms in 1995.

Drug Task Forces seemed to be putting a dent in illegal drug labs in subsequent years, but between 2007 and 2009, meth seizures increased 87%. In February, 2012, Mexican authorities made just one bust of over 15 tons of it. Tremendous profits could be earned selling the relatively easy to produce street drug. In late 1998, the "Contreras Family Operation", a meth ring which ran out of San Bernardino, California, netted an estimated $100,000 dollars a month.2

The Green Dragons in New York and the Black Dragons in San Francisco are known to have smuggled in "China White" which was considered a "Cadillac drug" on the street. Heroin came back into heavy use again in the mid-90s, especially Mexican Black Tar. Post-Punk and Grunge rock bands made the drug very popular amongst youth. Homeless white kids by the hundreds could be found walking the University of Washington District, Belltown, or along Broadway on Seattle's

Capitol Hill to score some "H". In 1992, 8% percent of adult admissions to all publicly funded treatment programs in Seattle were for heroin. By 1996, the figure had grown to 14%. While much of Europe gets heroin from Afghanistan, the majority of U.S. heroin still came from Mexico. Street kids were overdosing practically every weekend shooting up the ever-potent "Mexican Black Tar Heroin". Hispanic gangs from Mexico and L.A. brought much of it up. I found a vast majority of Hispanic inmates are in fact booked on drug charges. Domestic violence was number two, followed by driving violations. Many were undocumented workers who were unemployed at the time. For them dealing drugs was not exactly their ticket to freedom and prosperity. Many times, they were "fronted" small portions of heroin from a bigger dealer when they were "popped by police" trying to sell it. The new craze was then Oxycontin.3

Now, the latest epidemic is Fentanyl. To see the damage that is being done to people and our communities with this drug that is causes overdoes and deaths in record numbers see "Broken Dreams" on YouTube.

The drug problem also affected our neighbors south of the border. According to Dr. Julio Amador, formerly with the Baja California Coroner's Office, "the majority of guns in Mexico are smuggled in by Americans. Mexico has very strict gun laws unlike the U.S." 4

 In 1998, there were one hundred twenty-three U.S. citizens arrested for violating its "Firearms and Explosives Act". Americans loved their guns and street gang members loved them even more. The "Operation Fast & Furious" scandal showed big problems with "gun walking".

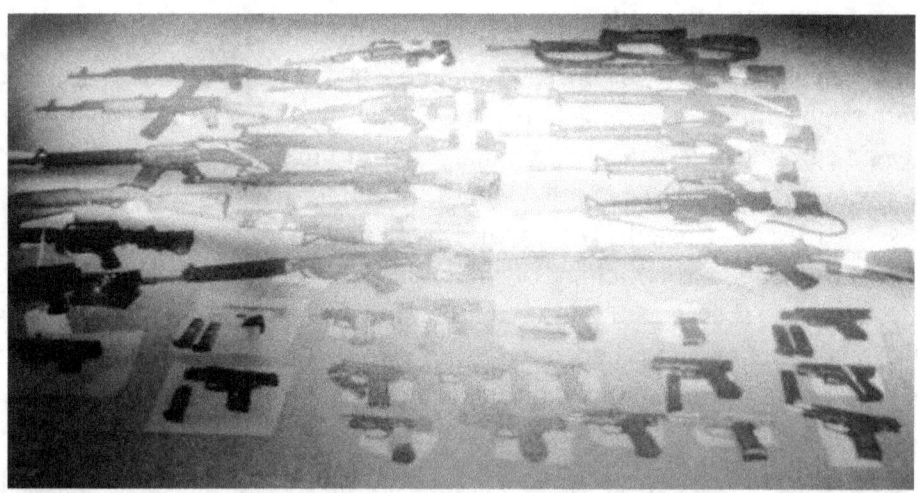

Gang members say, "If you want to protect your business, you had better have back-up weapons". Dope dealers constantly have to watch their backs, not only for the police, but even more so for people looking to rip them off. Often these drug dealers will reach out to others for protection from rip-offs. Dealers are also often forced to pay taxes on the street to prison gangs for protection in order to operate in their areas. It's a rough lifestyle.

You always have to look over your shoulder. Many inmates incarcerated on assault charges have told me, "I got off first!" meaning they shot someone because they felt it was imminent that their rivals would shoot them.

Most shootings are not random. Gang members frequently use high powered firearms. Drive-by shootings sometimes thought to be a phenomenon of the 1990's street gang culture were really first used in the early 1920s by the Capone Gang and other criminal groups. A drive-by shooting occurs where members from one gang seek out the homes, business, vehicles, or hangouts of their rivals. By using weapons, they will "drive by" and shoot at the rival member. Sometimes, the "suspect" member will taunt, yell, or shout the attacking gang's name or slogan so that the "victim" is challenged to retaliate, often conducting a payback shooting within 24 hours.

In 1992, there were 803 gang related homicides, and in 1997 there were 450 gang-related deaths in the Los Angeles County. Much of it was a result of drug or gang turf wars.5

A prime factor in the rise of gang violence during the 1980s and 1990s was the mass marketing of high-capacity semiautomatic pistols such as 9mm handguns with large ammo clips, these quickly became gang favorites. The proportion of Los Angeles County gang homicides in which semiautomatic pistols were used skyrocketed. This heightened firepower also dramatically increased the likelihood that someone, not necessarily the intended target, would be hit by one of the rounds sprayed out during increasingly popular drive-by shootings. As gang shootings rose, so did the fear that caused many kids to join gangs for protection.

According to a reliable source as of June 1, 2008, there were 7,703 gangs and 223,828 gang members in California's CAL-GANG database. At the same time, information on the firearms used in youth gang violence often fails to give an accurate picture and now with many agencies not even entering into CAL-GANG it is even more difficult. It is often hard to know what crimes were gang related and which were not in compiled gang statistics. Different jurisdictions not only define gangs differently, but also what constitutes a "gang related crime". Often in shootings one or more persons involved were gang members but the crime stat is chalked up as being personal or domestic violence related. Despite the large amount of information being collected by most police departments a very limited amount of information is released to the general public that can be applied to understanding the role that firearms play in youth gang violence.

Police know that when a drive-by occurs, the victims will usually want revenge. That is the critical time to show police presence, use open communication, and to convince the targets to utilize the criminal justice process. Juveniles were murdered at the rate of seven per day in the U.S. in the 1990s, much of it tied to the drug trade.6

Gunshot violence costs over 20 billion dollars a year. A good percentage of this cost goes to medical expenses for victims who cannot afford insurance so the public ends up paying the bill. The Federal Center for Disease Control estimated in the year 2003 death by guns replaced death by auto accidents as the number one reason for unnatural death among young people, especially with young Black and Latino men.7

Teens today can easily get stolen guns for 50 to 100 bucks. It's easier to get a gun than it is to get a car. You can't buy rifles or shotguns in Washington until age 18. People can possess a pistol in limited circumstances at 18, but can't purchase one or carry a concealed pistol until age 21. But teens unable to get a handgun legally often just ask around on the streets until they're connected with street dealers who specialize in selling firearms. Sometimes they peddle a range of guns right out of the trunks of their cars.8

The race for firearms is not only limited to just the barrios and ghettoes, but has spread into suburban communities, quiet towns, and schoolyards. Suburbanites were stunned and caught off guard when the Littleton, Colorado, shooting happened in April of 1999. Fifteen victims, including the two shooters were killed.

Today, few places in the U.S. are really safe. Residents of the barrio may feel like hostages in their own neighborhoods. There may be bars on the windows which can make a home resemble a jail. Freeway signs may have barbed wire wrapped around them so they don't get "tagged". There is constant gunfire echoing and police helicopters buzzing over at night. The area can resemble a war zone. As if the physical appearance of the neighborhood is not bad enough, the emotional price on families from the effects of "Varrio Warfare" can be devastating. People of the barrio might really wonder if they're not actually in Bosnia or Baghdad or Afghanistan. To many young people in the barrio, it's safer to join a gang than be caught without your Homies.

Many children are afraid to cross varrio lines spelled out in the graffiti marking the area as gang turf. The price for wearing the wrong color of clothing can mean a severe beating or worse. The wrong answer to, "What varrio are you from?", can mean instant death.

The result of years of violence in Latino communities has taken its toll in the barrio. There are dozens of people that have been crippled by gang warfare in virtually any given place in America. The life span of a gang member can be very short. Cemeteries are full of tombstones marked "Rest in Peace". Funerals can become almost commonplace to teenagers. Mothers weep for their kids at night wondering if they'll come home. Innocent children can be caught up in the violence of rival gangs. 9

Young Eduardo Samaniego was one such boy. He had witnessed a homicide by members of "Pomona's 12th Street Gang". He dreamed of being a big league baseball player, only to have his dreams cut short by a murderer.

The following page has names of just a few of the people killed in the Northwest U.S. 2010-11 as a result of gang violence. Some of the victims were gang affiliated themselves, but not all. The suspects or convicted killers were all believed to be gang members:

Fernando "Scarface" Figueroa, 21-years-old

Luis "Loco" Gonzales, 32-years-old

Samuel Cruz Villegas, 29-years-old

Manuel "Mr. Trippy" Garcia, 28-years-old

David R. Duarte, 40-years-old

Carlos "Vago" Leyva, 17-years-old

Alex "Baby Puppet/ Plex" Ixta, 15-years-old

Juan "Snapper" Zuniga-Gonzalez, 26-years-old

Jorge "Payaso" Cuevas, 29-years-old

Daniel Rivera, 18-years-old

Julio Cervantes, 17-years-old

Raul Madrigal, 18-years-old

David Baldonado, 15-years-old

Arturo "Downer" Delarosa, 20-years-old

Edwin "Chow" Cesar-Davalos, 19-years-old

Alejandro Cisneros, 20-years-old

Arthur "Boo" Banda, 19-years-old

River Saenz, 21-years-old

Ariel "Sniper" Velasco, 16-years-old

Ruben Mata, 32-years-old

Danny Valenzuela, 21-years-old

Alejandro "Sniper" Baldavinos, 27-years-old

Joaquin O. Serrano, 23-years-old

Adan Beltran, 25-years-old

Diana Lopez, 16-years-old

Julio "Cartoon" Cesar-Martinez, 20-years-old

Alfredo Arredondo, 17-years-old

Ramon Mejia-Cono, 22-years-old

Luis "Yapperz" Martinez, 18-years-old

Ramiro Munoz Jr., 40-years-old

Mario "Raskal" Calvillo-Ramirez, 27-years-old

Raymond "Mr. Lil Man" Flores, 31-years-old

Julio "Stoner" Cesar Marquez, 13-years-old

Mariano "Travieso" Cuevas, 18-years-old

Chapter 8

Classification and Counseling

When an inmate goes to jail or prison, one of the first staff persons they speak with is likely to be a Classification Specialist who assesses inmate needs vs. institutional needs. Effective Classification can reduce escapes and escape attempts, suicides and suicide attempts, and inmate assaults and assault attempts.

Classification systems are a relatively recent addition to institutional management. In the "old days" when an inmate came into a corrections facility, they were often housed by being thrown in all together regardless of their charges or potential safety and security threat. The convict tank bosses ruled. Needless to say, this system did not work very well. The history of inmate classification in the United States closely parallels the evolution of the nation's correctional philosophy. Prior to 1870, when corrections focused on retribution and punishment, classification was primarily based on the type of criminal offense and inmates were classified per "appropriate punishment" to the crime. In the latter part of the nineteenth century; however, corrections changed direction, introducing reform and rehabilitation as important goals.

The treatment trend continued for about 100 years, well into the 1970s, when "rehabilitation" started to lose its appeal and retribution once again became a favored model. Public outrage and frustration over rising crime rates, the increasing numbers violent offenders, and the perceived failure of these programs to actually "correct" criminal behavior all contributed to the swing of the "correctional pendulum". Victim restitution started to gain support as part of a judge's sentencing options. These treatment versus security concerns are still issues with correctional counselors today. Juvenile institutions still tend to use the rehabilitation model, but even this may be changing. For instance, in King County, Washington, the juvenile detention system was under the "Department of Youth Services", but is now called the Department of Adult and Juvenile Detention.

Washington state youth facilities still fall under the "Juvenile Rehabilitation Administration" of the State Department of Social and Health Services. Most delinquent youth that fall under authority of juvenile justice system are deemed more appropriate and amenable for counseling. Intervention and group counseling techniques may work well for this group. Adult prisons may offer treatment facilities for a few who are a low security risk for such programs. The initial classification of these offenders in prison can be based on a review of court paperwork, diagnostic tests, criminal profile treatment categories, and a "points" category system.

There are three main theories about why some people are more prone to commit crimes than others: Physiological, in that some persons may be pre-determined to commit their offenses based on defective genes or organic brain damage. Psychological, based on the personality of the individual that is a direct result of the way a toddler is reared. Sociological, by the way society influences a juvenile as they are growing into adulthood.

All of these theories have been studied and discussed by the experts in the field with varying amounts of accuracy found according to the research conducted and statistics gathered thus far. It's not perfect science.

In the 1980-90s, the correctional philosophy leaned back towards a system based upon "retributive punishment" but still often provided opportunities for those who program or comply with the rules and regulations. Subjective classification relies upon informal criteria that can lead to inconsistencies, biases, or error in staff decision making with potential legal liabilities. Objective classification systems are the most widely used system today. It depends on a narrow set of well-defined (and legally defensible) personal characteristics. These categories are often based on the seriousness of current offense, detainer status or holds from other jurisdictions, prior violent offenses, escapes, age, and amount of prison terms served. Inmate behavior while incarcerated (probably the most important) is used to further classify an offender by management risk. This helps ensure that classification is an effective risk management tool with the goal of placing the offenders in the least restrictive custody designation while still meeting the need to provide safety and security for the public.

Several factors can keep classification and correctional systems from operating as intended. Among the more common areas are: Few inmate programs, lack of diverse housing environments, chronic overcrowding, lack of adequate or grossly inadequate training for staff, no existing standards for proper classification, and insufficient behavior tracking data. Corrections staff may be taught to be "reactive not proactive". This can be due to a poorly run administration, weak management practices, lack of quality leadership and vision, or not living up to the department's mission statement. Nationally, over 65% of inmates are classified and housed as medium or maximum security. Many times, inmates are classified as medium security and just "warehoused" which does not encourage good behavior nor do a very good job of punishing poor behavior. In other words, there are few meaningful incentives for programming and few sanctions or punishments for unruly prisoners.

Classification aimed at identifying and managing inmates who present a threat to the secure, safe, and orderly operation of the facility can also be rendered almost useless by the physical design of the facility itself. In some facilities, inmates are classified and housed within a facility according to their past offense history and current offense. Inmate felons separated from misdemeanors, violent from non-violent charges, etc. Today, professionals working in the business know that large jail systems must contend with the high volume of daily inmate admissions. It often becomes a juggling act. Many jails have certain cells designed for maximum security, rendering futile the categorization by different custody levels. Some jails are under court order, such as the "Hammer Decision" in Seattle, to reduce overcrowding. For this reason, many county and city jails have built new direct supervision facilities, at less cost per inmate.

A lot of problems in prisons or jails can be solved by good Interpersonal Communication skills. Whether working in a direct or indirect facility, staff should be "Firm, Fair, and Consistent". Being visibly upset, yelling, or overreacting often plays into the offender's penchant for manipulation. These individuals are experts at knowing what human reaction or behavior will be reciprocated and will attempt to intimidate, undermine programs, or produce sympathy and camaraderie amongst their peers. "Peer pressure" or "playing inmates against inmates" can backfire. This is the "tank boss" philosophy. At the same time, staff cannot be perceived as being weak. When I speak to inmates, I always give an ounce of dignity and usually get a pound of respect in return.

Sometimes the offender can be motivated to accept help by confronting them about their problems and getting them to change their attitudes about life. I see this sometimes in older more mature offenders. Sometimes they find religion and get a spiritual reawakening. I try to help them think about others more than themselves. Even where there are good programs available, one of the problems in treating individuals in the Criminal Justice system may be that the offender is in denial or has no real conscience about what they have done. There is some direct scientific evidence that pre-natal care is a major factor in whether a person fully grows and develops as a mature adult or can be developmentally disabled for life. I can't tell you how many times I've had an individual in my office on drug charges with numerous drug convictions. When I ask them if they have a drug problem they state, "No", with big open ugly abscesses visibly showing. Or they say, "My only problem is I don't have any (drugs)."

In this situation treatment is unlikely to help without them first realizing or wanting to change the problem. It is very hard to reach somebody in denial or who does not have the mental capacity to be aware. I have also seen this effect in younger inmates whose mothers drank alcohol during pregnancy (fetal-alcohol syndrome) and in the drug addicted (ex. crack babies) inmates who grew up in the system. They break society's laws and even in custody they break rules and may have no real idea why. The majority of offenders I interview have not had a functional family. Either the mother or the father (or both) have substance abuse problems. Many had teenage mothers who themselves had little child rearing experience. The grandparents often try to raise the grandkids during the parent's absence or while they are in jail in the hopes of preventing Child Protective Services from taking the kids away, but often they did not have the time, energy, or resources to give the children attention they really need. The child may grow up being angry at the parents and take it out on the world.

Offenders who I interview often lack any responsibility and will not own up to their behavior. They place the blame on society and state they were dealt a bad deck of cards. There was nothing to do in the hood. They do not see the opportunity for success or advancement in their environment. Youth from a lower class neighborhood may lack the job skills, education, and social "connections" for advancement. Minority youth may feel labeled or feel little self-worth. There is, in fact, often more crime problems in the barrio. Youth may be pulled over more in traffic stops and feel harassed by the police. They may be prosecuted more often with less financial opportunities to get a good lawyer. They may be assigned a public defender who may argue for a guilty plea bargain. They see many minority youth just like themselves locked up and may identify with the outlaw and drug culture. They may feel hopeless and may feel they are destined to end up in jail or prison.

Lack of available bed space frequently leads to "capacity-driven" classification decision making or "just having a warm body to fill a bed" and often leads to more hopelessness. Housing and program assignments are determined not by formal policies and procedures set in place nor by inmate needs, but by the available bed space and program openings in a unit. Classification is used to meet the facilities' needs rather than the inmate's program eligibility. Management may face local political pressure to ensure "perceived public safety" and restrict inmates to the highest security level or, in some cases, stress the rights of inmates to the least restrictive level without merit. Caseloads may be so heavy that the classification unit may only see the offender briefly at intake and briefly before release. Female inmates may be subject to a high number of lower security overrides while the males, especially minorities, may face more classification overrides to maximum security levels.

There may be an unspoken gang identification policy of "Don't ask, don't tell." I sometimes have a hard time changing this attitude amongst line staff, supervisors, and especially management. While Security Threat Groups nationwide only make up on average between 5% and 15% of the total inmate population that they generate approximately one third of the disciplinary infractions and are involved in over 50% of the fights or "code blues". In addition, very few departments have a good computer tracking system of disruptive individuals and gang members who tend to be much more sophisticated at manipulating classification and disciplinary action. Most staff, especially Administration, don't live in areas of high gang problems so just don't see the damage they can do. They may also be uneducated or unwilling to see the damage gangs do inside facilities.

They may feel if they pay attention to gangs then they may be seen as somehow giving them power they do not deserve. I have also heard Administration state that if you document gangs and they get into a fight or create a disturbance then they might sue and claim you knew about it beforehand. Failure to act and deliberate indifference to these issues are a greater liability in my professional opinion.

This happened with the Calvin Hammer lawsuit in King County. To this day, it is has one of the biggest effects on the King County Jail, and they're still paying. In 1988, an inmate named Calvin Hammer got in a fight, and the bones in his face were broken. He sued. Many years later, the incident was a big reason why the county closed some of its parks for lack of funding. Hammer's injuries, the mishandling of his treatment, and subsequent court settlement led to stringent controls over medical services provided King County Jail inmates and at much higher costs. In 2002, the county's cost for correctional health and rehabilitation services was $22.5 million dollars. That was more than the $18 million a year it cost to run all county parks.

I agree, not all gang members need to be segregated. Rather a "get along" approach should be encouraged. But disruptive individuals of Security Threat Groups should be identified, verified, and housed according to their management risk. More programs should be available to those inmates who behave while incarcerated.

Sometimes the unit officer won't work with the classification officer and visa-versa to monitor the progress of an individual inmate for proper reclassification. Some officers may insist on moving inmates to other areas without prior approval or classification or just pass problem inmates on to another unit without addressing problems. If there are enemies or "keep separate" issues, there may be some potentially big libelous situations, but you have to check. Temporary administrative segregation and isolation from the general population until the unit classification or disciplinary officer can reevaluate the inmate's status may limit some of these problems.

The majority can later be released to general population to a program that will help the inmate succeed.

It is also important to remember that while chain gangs and hard labor have regained popularity in some parts of the country, most of these people will be getting out one day. Some corrections officials believe they must only take a tough stance and brand any kind of treatment just "coddling criminals". Yes, meaningless programs or treatment only makes a mockery out of the whole system, but I believe we should be caring and expect strict accountability. These people will need to know better social and job skills besides drug dealing or preying on innocent victims upon their re-entry to society or they will probably be destined to fail again and become part of the "revolving door". We need to be tough on crime, but also be smart about crime and its causes.

Non-institutional counselors and social workers that deal with gang members must understand their clientele.

While it is not absolutely necessary to understand the Spanish language when dealing with Hispanic offenders it helps to have at least a working knowledge of the language. "Conversational Spanish" college courses may be best. Some regions offer short courses that may assist you also. Remember that many offenders will speak "street Spanish or calo slang". It is important to know certain code words, which may be warning signs.

Hispanic offenders may also use body language and hand expressions which can indicate where they are coming from. I believe understanding the culture will assist a counselor in offering better services to their client.

You'll notice, I have not included a lot of "empirical studies" or taken a "clinical approach" here to back up my conclusions. Although I could easily come up with lots of statistics to prove my claims via "evidence based" numbers. What I have done is conduct thousands of interviews with gang experts, staff, and inmates and included that information here for you to read. I did a lot of reading and networking with service providers too.

I am not perfect, so yes, I have been known to be "erroneous" at times as has any other person who takes some risks with judgment calls, conceptions, or beliefs. Educated opinions and debates about these problems are healthy. I am constantly reevaluating the gang situation and listen to other respected figures in my field because the situation is constantly evolving and changing. I wasn't born in the sticks of Montana, I didn't learn about Latino gangs, violence, and varrios in a book or in a gang class. While I took classes in college on English 101, psychology, and criminal justice, I found you can learn more from people just by watching and listening to them with an open mind.

I read offender statistics every day, but my main credibility and experience comes from dealing with gangs while growing up, from shotcallers at Folsom while working the front lines in the street, jail, and prison. I personally escorted Joe Morgan, Honorary Godfather of the Mexican Mafia and dealt with former members. I read hundreds of gang debriefs to understand why some individuals acted a certain way. I spoke many times with x-NF heavies like General "Babo" Sosa and other drop-outs. I was there watching carefully while the Bulldogs were evolving and barking in the housing units. I often learned the hard way. Many times, I feared for my safety and wasn't always sure I'd come home at night.

Over the years I've learned how to deal with the inexperienced juvenile gang member and offenders to the sophisticated prison gang member and dangerous convict. I've learned how to counsel them and how to distinguish the hard-core offender with gang tats versus the ornamental tattoos that have become popular in recent years. For years, I studied prison art and tattoos that are easily identified by common symbols, prison towers, razor wire patterns, jail bars, clocks, sand time keepers, calendars, etc. and by their blueish-black ink that is often taken from staff pens. By using the motor from a radio as a tattoo gun or even a plain sowing needle to apply artwork or lettering to the skin. I checked how many are there and how big were the tattoos. It was usually an indication of how hard core a member is when they have big tattoos or write in large graffiti letters.

You won't have to ask them where they are from their varrio will be spelled out on their body for the whole world to see.

All of these clues helped me access what level of sophistication and how gang involved an individual was. As I tell my students in my gang classes, I've learned how to care, and you just can't teach that.

Some other questions to ask when making a gang assessment. Is their neighborhood gang controlled? The presence of lots of gang graffiti can be an indication of heavy gang activity in the area. Arriving at a proper conclusion entails making judgment calls based on the available background data, questions and answers, and reconfirmation of your decisions by monitoring behavior outcomes. You must gauge whether the client identifies with the Hispanic culture and to what extent. Don't just assume an offender identifies with the Latino culture just because he/she has a Spanish-surname or because he or she is dressed like a gang member. You must take a closer look.

Sometimes the parents or other family members were also involved with gangs. Is it a traditional extended Hispanic family? How supportive is the family of the offender? Treatment staff and case managers often make the complaint that clients improve while in a program only to relapse and revert to old habits upon completion, hence, some social workers and community service organizations prudently try to involve the whole family in treatment. This is particularly important when dealing with Hispanic groups, as the family value, whether functional or dysfunctional, is usually very strong. Try talking to other family members. Hispanic families are traditionally much extended with the grandparents, uncles, aunts, parents, and their children living in close proximity. In these families, the husbands went to work, the wives stayed home to have children and clean house. Like much of the rest of America this structure has changed. Both parents may be working due to financial hardship.

Many times, child rearing and quality contact is minimized. The child may be passive-aggressive or outwardly violent and act out in their frustration to get people to listen to their needs. Grandparents, aunts, and uncles may not be around to mentor. Roles may need to be clarified. Who is the father figure? Is he the only family disciplinarian? Is there a history of domestic violence within the family structure? Many times, especially among new Hispanic immigrant families there is machismo. I've barely touched on domestic violence issues here.

You should also take note. Does the family interact at the dinner table and are they involved in nurturing family functions? I believe that all people, no matter what culture, need to take care of

three things: The Mind, Body, and Spirit. How active is the family in religious activities or how strong are spiritual beliefs? How can the church or volunteer religious service worker assist you in behavior modification? All of these factors and resources can assist in helping you determine how strong the offender's support network is. One must look at the big picture and utilize all available resources.

Research has also shown that visitation and assessments by social workers to at-risk families can reduce youth violence by almost half. Lack of family ties, no strong role models, economic deprivation, cultural alienation, lack of attention, boredom, substance abuse, poor education, peer pressure, and fear of violence can all help cause a young person to join a gang.1

Chapter 10

STOP THE VIOLENCE!

Gang Prevention

Now that we know what motivates somebody to join a gang and how different gangs operate, how do we prevent them? In any gang prevention program there are certain indicators that first need to be identified and assessed. Youth may have a dysfunctional family structure, show low motivation, are easily angered, have little interest in school, or have no occupational goals. They may also exhibit signs of drug and alcohol use. Many schools, social workers, and police have seen that prevention can work to counteract the negative effects of gangs. Good gang prevention programs focus on self-change of the individual, not the gang. Prevention, as with intervention, must offer positive alternatives to the gang lifestyle.

It used to be that when kids got in trouble and were expelled from school they were just "passed on" to another school. Many counselors are now avoiding "passing the buck" and keeping these delinquents out of traditional classrooms by steering them towards alternative schools. Lack of discipline in the classroom prevents non-gang kids from learning too. Public school districts who haven't "overreacted" have hired more Security Officers to deal with the problem while respecting student's rights. Metal detectors have been installed in many inner city schools. This can ease fears of non-gang kids and prevent weapons from entering the school grounds. Even suburban schools are looking to prevent crime gangs, and track problem students better, especially in the wake of the Columbine High School Massacre and subsequent mass shootings.

Parents, Teachers, Social Workers, and Criminal Justice Personnel, must work with all elements of the system in order for it to work more effectively:

Social Service Agencies

Family

Schools	Prevention	Parole
Juvenile	Intervention	Prison
Probation	Suppression	Jails

Police

Criminal Justice Components

Note: The Courts may intervene at most Levels)

Some communities and politicians have tried to prevent warring gangs from fighting by bringing them together. This occurred in Central America in April, 2012, when the Church arranged a truce between the Mara Salvatrucha and 18th Street gangs. Many people have asked me about my feelings about gang truces to prevent violence. After the Rodney King Riots, referred to by some radical elements as an "Uprising", many members of the Crips and Bloods decreased warfare against each other. What many people do not know is they did not stop criminal activities. They just focused crimes more on the general public.

One Pomona veterano told me, "We used to hang out at Sharkey Park on Grand Avenue and they used to hang out at Cherryville Park on Hamilton. Our gang would agree to meet with their gang in neutral Ralph Welch Park and play Turkeybowl football on Thanksgiving Day. But, after the game, it was back to gang-banging."1

While well intentioned, truces may stop gangs from committing crimes against each other but may not necessarily deter crime. Programs and approaches that aren't closely monitored generally will not work. The National Gang Center attempts to bring the various prevention components to work together and has an internet gang discussion group. In 2001, the City of Houston, Texas, under guidance from the Mayor's Office and skilled youth workers like Victor Gonzalez and his team, started a project known as "Gang Free Schools". Summer Schools are good too. Recreational opportunities provided by the "Salvation Army, Boys & Girls Clubs, and YMCA" all have proven to be effective by occupying a youngster's idle time and preventing gangs. The kids belong to a group which also promotes, exercise, good health, and nourishment.

Another good program that seems to work are Police Athletic Leagues (PAL's). Many police departments have "D.A.R.E.", "G.R.E.A.T.", and "Youth at Risk" programs that work with Community Oriented Policing (COP). The Seattle Police Department considers kids who show early gang involvement to be youth at risk. The COP philosophy entails getting as many community agencies and residents as possible to be involved in order to take back their neighborhoods.

Curfews, After-School programs, "Neighborhood Watch", "Nights Out", graffiti eradication, garbage removal, etc. can show that people care about the area. The "Broken Windows" theory, first proposed by noted political scientists James Q. Wilson and George L. Kelling, argues that broken windows and potholes in roads tell hoodlums that, "people just don't care". Change doesn't happen overnight but what is clear is that the whole community must get involved. It's the old adage, "An ounce of prevention is worth a pound of cure!"2

Out on the street, Foot and Bicycle Patrols are another way to improve inter-personal communications. Officers should remember most of the victims and witnesses of gang violence live in the same communities as the perpetrators.

Crime Prevention hasn't always been a big concern in Corrections. Many of the older types of prisons and jails in the U.S. were built with blind spots where it was hard for Correctional Officers to see. Some facilities had to be restructured. For instance, the McNeil Island Prison originally built between 1872 and 1875 in Washington State was taken over from the Feds in 1982. It practically had to be rebuilt, but closed for good in 2011. Today prisons are designed with safety, security, and violence prevention in mind. As we discussed in Chapter 8, for properly classified inmates, direct supervision facilities are a great improvement over housing offenders in the old linear tier system or even the more modern pod unit system. In direct supervision, the officer practically lives with the inmates. There are no physical barriers to separate the officer from the inmate. Interpersonal communication skills can be used to prevent problems from occurring, but you must talk to the offenders and have a good rapport. This can prevent a lot of violence from happening out on the street or behind the walls.3

Intervention

If a gang problem already exists, then direct intervention is needed. This is probably the most difficult, least tried, and less appreciated approach to work with gangs. It addresses kids already involved but not too far gone.

Again, the first step of action is for parents, schools, local city and county governments to get out of the "denial syndrome" in order to effectively deal with it. Many public institutions such as the schools, police, city hall, county councils, and even the church are now seeing that gangs are everybody's problem and we cannot afford to just pass the buck as in years past. Even a few doctors have volunteered their time with tattoo removal programs. Gang members who want to turn their life around and try to get a job may have a hard time because of their tattoos. Who would want to hire someone like that?

Father Greg Boyle of Dolores Mission Parish in East L.A. has some success at "Homeboy Industries", an economic development program started in 1992. He found that many gang members couldn't find a job so he created a job, trained them at a skill, and began referring them to local employers. The slogan of "Build Jobs, Not Jails!" and "Nothing Stops a Bullet like a Job!" has caught on with the homeboys of the varrio. He says, "We need more of these intervention programs. You can't pick and choose. Will it be prevention or suppression? We have to do it all!"4

José Gallegos is a Gang Intervention Specialist who grew up in a Compton barrio in L.A. County. He's worked hard to hook kids up with the independent living skills and support systems they will need to become successful. In more recent years he worked as a Vice Principal and mentored to kids at Dominguez High School in Compton. He states, "It's a tough sell, but many people only look at the negative stuff with gang members. Not all are doing the negative stuff; the majority do have positive qualities. We must intervene and focus on them being involved in positive things."5

According to Youth Counselor Delfino Muñoz with Seattle's Proyecto Saber Program, "The first step is to notify parents that that Juanito or Juanita is engaging gang-types of activities. Our experience shows that gang members come from all kinds of families. If the parent is in denial, a counselor may be assigned to the kid".6

Albino Garcia is an ex-addict from Chicago worked with the "Barrios Unidos Program" in Santa Cruz, California. He states, "I know the gang mentality is that everyone who is not in the gang is the enemy. This only breeds anti-social behavior. Gang members tend to go back to violence when they are in danger. It is fight or flight. At Barrios Unidos we teach them about 'GANAS' how to be a warrior. We teach them about basic human relationships, spirituality, and non-violent approaches to their problems." 7

Cook Barrett of the Albany, New York, Gang Prevention Program, works with the city's young people, preventing youth gangs, and fostering partnerships that that support crime prevention efforts. The goal of the program is the development and implementation of a coordinated community response to the youth gangs. This approach involves four main strategies: community building, education, peer mentoring, and employment preparedness. The mission of the program is to coordinate a comprehensive mechanism to reduce gang-related crime and deter youth from joining gangs. Cook often intervenes and parts with words of wisdom for kids such as telling them, "When you want something you've never had, you have to do something you've never done." 8

Personally, I've also always encouraged kids to get involved in culture, art, or writing as a positive experience, and have talked to kids at the King County Juvenile Detention facility for years. I also talked to kids in L.A. and other parts of the United States. I recall several youngsters that I tutored in Yakima at the Southeast Community Center way back in the early 1980s. They were from a farmworker family and were not doing well at school since they often had to help their family work. Several of them were showing signs of gang involvement. The parents did not speak English and had little idea of what the kids were up to. I took them under my wing and got them to help me paint a mural, write poetry, and finish their homework. I could tell from the smiles on their faces that they enjoyed it and that it made them think about the direction they were heading in life.

While I was a peer counselor and supervisor with the Seattle Summer Youth Employment Program back in the 1970s, I taught carpentry skills to troubled youth from the projects. Many of them previously only knew how to destroy things. Several of them had vandalism charges on their records. Negative or not, gangs met their own needs in the past. I connected with them, acknowledged them as human beings, opened up communication, and reinforced "choices and consequences". They took great pride in building and refurbishing park playgrounds for their younger siblings. For some of them it was the only accomplishment they felt they did in a long time.

We all must steer kids towards legitimate goals and personal growth opportunities and lead by example.

Without positive guidance in my life, I too could have easily become a statistic. I also remember when the "Scared Straight" approach was used to intervene. Back in the 1970s, there were riots in prisons across America. There was Attica, which ended in a violent takeover by law enforcement and U.S. National Guard troops. The Sante Fe Riot in 1980 resulted in the death of thirty-three prisoners and caused over 28 million dollars in damage. Inmates actually ran many prison programs in "Concrete Mama". Some of these were legitimate self-help programs; others were just "fronts" for illegal activities. While prisons can still be unpleasant and violent places, most have now been redesigned (as discussed earlier) to help prevent violence.9

The kids I see are growing up much faster on the street today. They are exposed to much greater violence on the screen and in real life. While a "Scared Straight" or "Boot Camp" programs may still have benefits for some, many of the kids I talk to today have actually told me they feel safer being locked up. Jail and prison is not the deterrent it once was to scare kids. Today, most jails operate safely, securely, and humanely. For several decades now, I've helped offenders get into programs, be it worker or job training, education, life skills, drug and alcohol classes. I've made psych and medical referrals. I've also noticed many offenders perform well in a controlled environment, but have problems transitioning that discipline and structure to the street.

There are some intervention programs such as Group Homes, Pre-Release, Work Release, and Re-Entry, but these are not always mandatory. In many states there are long waiting lists because of crowded conditions.

Technically speaking, you can have a Maximum Security inmate come out of a highly controlled isolation cell in prison, locked down 23 hours a day, given their "release money", and sent off on a bus for a home they hardly know. They may be "high control" or high-risk community security. Although banned from associating with felons, many start out good at first then soon begin to backslide with the old gang and back to bad habits. Parole programs attempt to protect the public and assist parolees in their reintegration into society and attempt to keep tabs on progress of the parolee and decide if they need returned to prison if they violate conditions.

One of the most important gauges of the need to intervene whether on the street or in lock-up is the correlation between active gang members, crimes committed, and behavior. I monitored Security Threat Group member and Disciplinary data on a daily basis. All data I've found suggests that gang members commit a significant number of crimes when compared to non-gang affiliated persons.10

Professional groups like the American Jail Association and the American Correctional Association review programs and classification systems to better handle violent offenders. Again, whether inside or out it's very important to intervene before the gangs do.

Suppression

Sometimes outright suppression or force is the only way to fight the gangs. Situations like this would be where life or extreme property damage is involved to protect public safety and general order. The suppression strategy seeks to identify, track, and target individuals and gangs until they are locked up or are run out of the area.

Suppression tactics can take place in many forms. Where delinquent gangs are present, truancy laws for schools and juvenile curfew laws can be enforced. Where gangs spray-paint graffiti, individuals who continuously vandalize property can be targeted for prosecution. There can be increased penalties for felons carrying firearms. Where gangs deal drugs certain "Stay out of Drug Area" (SODA) police sweeps can be effective. Prosecution under these drug charges carry enhanced sentences with intensive probation upon release. Sometimes, "Problem Oriented Policing" (POP) tactical units can target certain areas or known gang hangouts and try to prevent the gang from just moving across the street. The L.A. County Sheriff's Department targeted problem areas of the county "to stop the scourge of gang violence".

Operation Safe Streets gang units monitor criminal trends and activities. Many times, a Field Interview Report (FIR) is conducted. If a person continues to be involved in criminal activities, this contact can be used to build a case against them. They may be identified as a gang member, which can be introduced later in court to prove criminal intent. Gang members know this also and may file harassment claims. With suppression, one must be careful not to polarize the gangs.

For instance, in the early days of the fight against gangs in Los Angeles, law enforcement would often do sweeps in the barrio and lineup every youngster who fit the stereotype of a gangster look, i.e., young, minority, gang attire, lowrider, etc. This amounted to racial profiling. Some L.A. police officers also filled out FIRs with bogus or sketchy information that put the whole system at risk.

Many times, these kids were not involved in gangs but left with total disdain for the police after being held suspect and maybe more inclined to join. Gang members would say, "See how they do us ése!" The peripheral youth would become agitated and gravitate towards a gang. Years ago, while attending a community meeting that took place in the Valinda Corridor in the Eastside of L.A. County, I noticed crime goes up to a saturation level. Residents want the police to respond to every 911 call immediately. Police move in and start arresting the perpetrators. Crime recedes and residents see their sons being pulled over and confronted by the police.

Mothers cry harassment, community activists cry foul, lawyers threaten lawsuits, politicians intervene, and the police stop patrolling aggressively. The first level use of force is "presence". Crime starts to go up again because the gangsters know fewer police around to stop them. I have seen this cycle continue over and over again all over the U.S. often because lack of understanding by police and the community of each other's roles.

I've often heard police say, "I'm not a social worker. That's not my job!" Sometimes they even make offensive comments that make it very apparent that they despise and fear the community they are assigned to. The majority of their contacts in the area are of a negative nature. Their biases and prejudices are then reinforced.

Other officers, no matter what ethnicity, try to understand the area and the culture of the people they work with. They make their presence known and work very hard with the community to help set up community oriented police storefronts or substations and community outreach. I have heard residents speak very highly of them, even seek them, out and specifically ask the Chief or Sheriff to have them patrol the area.

Seattle Police Officer and later Chief of Police, Adrian Diaz, worked for many years as the department's Hispanic Community Liaison. He worked in a hard-pressed crime area of South Park with the help of neighborhood groups. Many violent crimes had occurred in the area, including gang related homicides. He worked with kids in after school programs at the local community center as well as in the schools in areas of Prevention and Intervention. He also worked to get some knuckleheads arrested and pulled off of the street. Diaz' efforts paid off and crime plummeted.

Gang problems can vary from city to city and activity can ebb or intensify due to a variety of factors such as the economy, gang wars, and police suppression efforts. In 1980, gang homicides numbered 351 in Los Angeles County, then went down to 205 in 1982, up to 803 during 1992, down to 450 in 1997, and only 297 in 2010. In Las Vegas, Nevada, gang murders totaled 90 in the year 2000, but crept up to 107 in 2012. A study done in Dallas, Texas, found curfew and truancy enforcement was very effective in reducing gang violence. Dallas Police Department targeted seven major street gangs and has educated parents and teachers to adopt zero tolerance. The City of Miami targeted five Hispanic gangs with its anti-gang initiative. Denver, Albuquerque, and other cities took similar action. 11

Other departments also documented and worked hard with politicians to create effective laws to suppress gangs. Police Department Gang Units have proven very effective in getting thugs off of the school grounds. Unfortunately, many gang units were reduced or eliminated later on due to budget cuts.

In 1993, the City of Chicago passed an anti-loitering law that helped remove many gang members from the street. The law was overturned by the State Supreme Court in the Morales Decision and in December of 1998 went to the U.S. Supreme Court. Currently, gang crime in Chicago is up.

In California, many cities have resorted to using street injunctions, a form of martial law to get chronic gang bangers off the street. These injunctions often ban targeted known gang members from "standing, sitting, walking, driving gathering or appearing anywhere in public view".12

Some groups like the American Civil Liberties Union (ACLU) were totally against gang injunctions and said they violated civil rights. Recently, many injunctions were ended. Only time will tell if gang violence creeps back.

Well timed use of force can sometimes prevent violence from erupting into a large-scale riot or from getting more people hurt. Examples of the progressive stages of use of force are: presence, verbal commands, soft hands, chemicals like "Pepperspray", baton, bean bags or wood blocks, and then lethal force. One of the most important accomplishments in the fight to suppress gangs was the "Street Terrorism and Prevention Act" (STEP) which became effective in California in 1986. But crime does not always stop once somebody is arrested as was covered in Chapter 4.

"Three-Strikes Laws" were aimed at getting repeat violent offenders off the street. Prior to the three-strikes laws, many states did have habitual offender laws but these were not as strongly worded as three-strikes measures. Other states have since passed similar laws which seem to be tough on crime; however, few states choose to prosecute often on three-strikes. The laws have taken away a lot of the discretion of the courts. Some judges are afraid of locking up prisoners for life as a potentially expensive way to deal with crime. It can be harder to convict inmates who generally will not plea-bargain with the prosecutor under three-strike rules. Many states have released former "Three strikes" inmates.

Suppression efforts in jail and prison are not just regulated to Corrections Emergency Response Teams (CERT) or Cell Extraction Teams. There should also be a good tracking of disciplinary problem inmates as well as gang members in correctional facilities to help suppress inmate on inmate and inmate on staff crime. Most corrections staff inside the institutions know it is important to not overreact to behavior and know when it is time to react or intervene. Some big city jails segregate gang leaders into a Security Housing Unit (SHU) or Administrative Segregation who have proven too violent to be housed in the general inmate population.

Many three-strikers were also hard-core gang members. The California Department of Corrections and Rehabilitation took active steps to deter violence. CDC(R) still has violent places, but assault rates have declined after several years of increases. To suppress the prison gangs, the agency created Security Housing Units (SHU). In 1995, the Department's assault rate dropped to one in 12,500 per day while in the early 1970s it was one in 1,200.16 Critics say the SHU is cruel and unusual punishment and recently there have been changes in SHU policy. Critics state it is all "smoke and mirrors". Again, reforms have changed the way many prisons operate and some SHUs were shut down or programs revised.

"Operation Safe Jails" was incorporated by the Los Angeles Sheriff's Department to teach gang members that have been housed in the L.A. County Jail gang modules to get along and intervene or suppress them if they don't.

At the King County Jail, when the L.A. gangs first started showing up in the mid-1980s, corrections officials tended to segregate gang members to prevent violence. It backfired and the gangs felt empowered. Today, many correctional agencies do not officially separate alleged or known gang members in different units. Isolation based on gang affiliation alone can form a power base for disruptive groups. It was found that this policy may empower the gangs and they can become more disruptive. However, different ethnic groups still tend to segregate themselves, which can cause racial tension in the units. Racial balance of units should be checked.

There has been a lot of public outcry, even amongst criminologists, that the system does not really do much "correcting". Some critics have argued that crowded prisons only lead to more violence to create more violent prisoners. 13

The Federal Bureau of Prison's statistics indicate that gang affiliated inmates are five times more likely to commit a serious violation of program rules, often with violence than a non-affiliated inmate. In 1994, the Federal Bureau of Prisons constructed its new supermax facility in Florence, Colorado. New "Super-Max or Ultra-Security" prisons were built for violent inmates who continue to commit horrendous crimes inside facilities. Except for boxer shorts and shower shoes, inmates in "the Max" can only have legal work, writing materials, and a small amount of hygiene items. Cell and strip searches are conducted often. All movement and privileges, including phone calls and recreational yard are severely limited. Inmates are locked down 23 hours a day. 14

When I worked the Violence Control Unit (VCU) and General Population (GP) as a Correctional Peace Officer on the yard at Folsom, many of the inmates would ask me to get the violent predators off of the yard. They wanted to program and wanted suppression too.

Chapter 11

Viewpoints on What Works

From 2006-2007, I served on the Washington State Gang Study Work Group via the Attorney General's Office and approved by the Governor. Our mission was to find out what works and what didn't work in addressing gang problems within the state. The end result was recommendations of some new laws that with put into place by politicians in Olympia, WA. It was a group of well intentioned and professional individuals but I was surprised most never had a Gangs 101 course.

From political and criminal justice examination over the years, we already know a lot about what doesn't work. New York's Tammany Hall in the late 1800s and early 1900s was corrupted by gangs, cops, and corrupt politicians discussed earlier in Chapter 1. Seattle and Vancouver during the 1950s had a vast network of police bribes and kickbacks.1

There are many in the Latino community today whose perception has not changed much about law enforcement. They refuse to even sit down with them and discuss the issues. On the other hand, many police unions have been resistant if not downright hostile to reforms. In Latin America, many police departments have a reputation for being corrupt. Pay is usually poor and some officers engage in "la mordida" or demanding bribes to squash any charges. Some law enforcement members in these countries have even worked for "death squads". People have great fear of being killed by the police there. Politicians may act in a state of lawlessness. It is little wonder that many people from other countries who live in the barrios do not hold American uniformed officers in the highest regard.

So, in order to have a police force that is less likely to be corrupted we have to pay them a decent living wage. We should not be defunding or abolishing the police, but there is room for improvement and better training and equipment is needed.

It is said, "Power and money corrupts", so we must keep them aware of new laws affecting their work and also help them from abusing their police powers.

What it really comes down to is how much law and order do we want? Some people prefer Anarchy and no rules or laws, but we cannot have a Police State either. It is a balancing act.

Any talk about the use of force or suppression cannot avoid the sensitive subject of "Police Brutality". This includes excessive use of force, as has been debated greatly since the not guilty verdicts against Los Angeles Police Department (LAPD) officers in April of 1992 Rodney King Riots and since the late 1990s Rampart Scandal. One of the cases involved police brutality against an African-American named Rodney King. Riots were sparked after a gang confrontation with "83 Crips" and widespread outrage that cops didn't play fair. Although many people felt there was a serious miscarriage of justice in the "Rodney King Case", most would not condone rioting about it.

The "Christopher Commission" investigation of LAPD after the riots found many problems within the force. The Rampart Scandal involved Rafael Perez and rogue cops abusing their authority and committing crimes. The televised beating of illegal immigrants by Riverside Sheriff's Deputies in 1996 and a shooting in 1997 of a young Black female also sparked mass protest in minority communities. In 2012, there was investigation into the "Jump Out Boys", a gang like group on the L.A. Sheriff's Gang Enforcement Team (GET). There was also a "3000" clique at the L.A. County Jail that used gang-like three-finger hand signs and earned their "3000" tattoo by breaking inmates' bones. Other cliques like Grim Reapers, Little Devils, Regulators, and Vikings, were accused of breeding a gang-like mentality in which deputies falsified reports and covered up misconduct.2

But these problems were not just limited to LAPD and the L.A. Sheriff's Department.

There are also abuse of force allegations in prisons and jails. The movie *"Felon"* is a fictional account of many of the problems. Police and Corrections critics applauded these reforms but are not often concerned with the effect of labeling on the force. At Corcoran State Prison in Central California, the question led to an investigation and reexamination into the shooting policy of the department.3

The arrest, use of force, and death of George Floyd in May 2020, was just another incident in a long string of high profile incidents that brought scrutiny of police tactics. Indeed, I believe there needs to be accountability of police and citizens. What is also dangerous is to tie the hands of corrections or law enforcement to do their job when the vast majority does act responsibly and are professional under extreme conditions. These are just some hot issues in criminal justice.

It was my experience as a training officer that the best time to monitor performance and gauge if one may be a future problematic officer is during their "probationary period". A thorough background check and many tests are given preceding a new candidate's employment. A psychological battery and lie detector test may also be given. However, screening racial or gender bias is rarely done in this process. I know from conducting these exams and sitting on oral boards that there are few questions dealing with this subject, in fact some of these tests and oral exams may be culturally biased. Lie detector tests are still used by some departments but not reliable. Sometimes, the Director or Chief has an unspoken mandate to find a particular kind of individual.

Cultural Awareness classes may be given at some point during training, but my experience shows that these classes are highly emotionally charged and largely inadequate. White males often feel they are blamed for past racism and minority candidates may have trouble even talking about past personal incidents because they do not want to be shunned or scorned by their peers. It might be better to have officers complete a college course on cultural awareness and sensitivity prior to employment? New staff may still be later taught by veterans to be against "care and treatment" to be "hard-ass and have a don't care attitude".

Once an officer passes probation it can be very difficult to fire them. The guilds and unions will often protect them no matter what the circumstances. Unions were created to protect workers from abuse and harassment from their employers, not to hide behind the badge or for a "Code of Silence". While the vast majority of officers wearing the uniform uphold the law and operate by ethics and morals worthy of a civil service employee, I think we need to admit a small fraction of staff have in fact crossed the line too many times from use of force to abuse of power and get rid of them with less union interference. They should understand that a poor police officer reflects badly on the group as a whole and in the eyes of the general public who hires them.

This danger has been with us since the beginnings of law enforcement. While many police departments are against "Citizen Review Panels" or "Inspector Generals", the public may perceive a cover-up unless allegations are thoroughly investigated by an independent body outside of the District Attorney's Office. Investigations by the DA's Office may be a conflict of interest since both departments are co-dependent on each other.

The U.S. Department of Justice (DOJ) Community Relations Service looks into alleged violations of the Civil Rights Act of 1964. Of course, staff are only human and all can have bad days when they do not react properly or are "off baseline". They DOJ should know this and not just be head hunters. But if we expect offenders not to use profanity, then neither should we on the job. We should be held accountable just as we expect to hold the violator accountable. Anything less would be hypocritical. Lack of professionalism undermines law enforcement and must be addressed early on in a career and long after the Academy.

As long as the public feels suppression is used as a last resort, it will continue to be an important tool in the fight against gangs and against all crime.

On March 29th, 2012, then Seattle Mayor Mike McGinn and then Police Chief John Diaz announced sweeping reforms in response to a highly critical federal Department of Justice report following a series of high-profile incidents involving people of color. As a result, 20 major reforms were proposed by the city and SPD brass that fell under 5 main categories: protecting constitutional rights; training for Seattle's values; earning public trust; using datadriven practices; and partnering with the public. The verdict is still out on whether the reforms will work long term?

Meanwhile, I must say it again, I still believe the vast majority of police do act professional and should be supported with their own programs to deal with the stress of the job. Law enforcement has had to step up its tactics in response to the gang's penchant for violence and assaults on officers. In 2010, 153 police officers were killed in the line of duty. In 2021, almost 450 were killed, 31% jump from 2020. Sometimes gang members would get "extra points" with their gang for killing an officer.4

We also need to ask ourselves the critical question, "Do we really want to win the drug war and at what cost?"

The "Drug War" has been going on for decades now. An increasing number of people are raising the taboo issue whether we should question this major American policy which has locked up tens of thousands of nonviolent offenders. Even former law enforcement officials like San Jose, California, Police Chief Joseph McNamara, have questioned if we are wasting our precious national resources. Looking at history, there are some striking resemblances to some of the side-effects that happened during "Prohibition" of alcohol. I am suggesting not so much to make hard drugs legal, but perhaps decriminalize it and treat it as a national health problem?

Drugs are often smuggled into correctional facilities. If someone is addicted, they will often go through extreme measures just to get a fix. Perhaps treatment for drug users would be a better policy? Drug courts are one good sentencing alternative idea. They are being used even in "get tough" states like Texas. Should "warehousing" of inmates be stopped and either force them to get into treatment and education programs or face more punitive action if they fail to do so? Are chain gangs and boot camps really effective? How do you stop an individual from being "institutionalized" when prison time is no longer a deterrent but viewed as a badge of honor? The public wants to lock criminals up but they don't want taxes raised to pay for it or build a prison in their area.

Over the years I have heard a lot of people also complain about the U.S. prison-industrial complex. Their comment that we lock up more people than most of the world has some merit. Many inmates feel there is not "equal justice under the law", especially when it comes to things like being able to hire an attorney versus getting a public defender.

The heated debate over gun control also continues. I am not anti-gun, but I don't belong to the NRA either. The Brady Bill addressed some gun issues but we must find more ways to get cheap handguns off the street. Several of the firearms used in the 1997 "North Hollywood Shootout" were purchased from gun shows. What use is a Tech-9 in a private collection except for bragging rights or to kill someone? Why does somebody need to own 200 guns? What kind of security do they have from would be gun thieves who can even break into gun stores?

To help curb the growth of gangs and related criminal activity, the FBI, at the direction of Congress, established the National Gang Intelligence Center (NGIC) in 2005. The NGIC integrates gang intelligence from across federal, state, and local law enforcement on the growth, migration, criminal activity, and association of gangs that pose a significant threat to the U.S. It supports law enforcement by sharing timely and accurate information and by providing strategic/tactical analysis of intelligence. Databases of each component agency are available to the NGIC, as are other gang-related databases, permitting centralized access to information. In addition, the center provides operational and analytical support for investigations. Using these resources, NGIC attempts to identify gangs that pose the greatest danger to our communities and targeted them with our combined investigative resources and the same federal racketeering statutes and intelligence and investigative techniques that have been used to attack organized crime. The NGIC is co-located with GangTECC, the National Gang Targeting, Enforcement, and Coordination Center, which is the national, multi-agency anti-gang task force created by the U.S. Attorney General. While the NGIC has been faced with funding cuts every year, many in law enforcement have seen it as the best answer for information on gangs located under one roof.

Louie Olivarez is a veteran police officer who grew up in the El Monte Flores varrio in Southern California and has seen the effects of gangs on the youth of today. He does have some tips. "Parents must know where their children are. Get the phone number of other parents. Kids may not like it, but, check up on them to see if they are really going to where they say they are going. Get them involved in school. We must not forget our spiritual and moral values. We must all work together to combat the problem. Most in law enforcement, have found that understanding and studying these groups' activities greatly increases stability in society." 5

Each community differs in gang development and violence levels so it needs different solutions. A combination of strategies that fits the community needs, and youth needs should be used to deter violence. Juanito who turned into "Capone" needs to be able to turn back into Juan. This can be done through counseling, mentoring, and schooling. Professional help can be sought out, community and faith-based organizations can provide alternatives to the gang lifestyle, and education and job training courses can be attended. Instead of being at war with themselves and the community, they may find inner peace, a peace that will be reflected in community.

We all must work together in this struggle if we want to see more success.

As most gang workers and police know, gang activity and gang crime is often a very hard thing to assess by looking at just statistics alone. The National Gang Center (NGC) website, formerly the National Youth Gang Center, states that it has a good analysis of "evidence based" findings. They also have nearly 15 years of data collected by their annual National Youth Gang Survey of 2,500 U.S. law enforcement agencies. Groups like the NGC focused on youth gangs, but not the vast majority of adult offenders that police crime and gang data bases (whether or not they admit they even exist for fear of legal issues) show are gang affiliated. This appeared to be a denial of some facts on the part of NGC and a big problem for communities when it comes to trying to get an accurate description of gang related issues they may be facing. I told then NYGC Director this and was met with hostility. While the NGC and major government funded groups like them do some real good work in many areas, the widely-circulated and relied upon gang information released from groups like them often controls subsequent government grant funding.

Some critics point out this so called evidence and stats generated by it can be skewed and misleading. Agencies may choose not to fill out surveys, do it incomplete, or enter info based on their own systems that may not be entirely accurate. Studies written on gangs are often based on this data and are often authored by college professors that have little to no hands on experience working with street gangs. It is often hard to match these academic studies with reality in the field. First of all, there is no gang definition or validation form that is standard nationwide. Different agencies define gang members differently. Competing data systems like GANGNET and RISS do exist. This can lead to discrepancies in reports on levels of gang activity which are often relied upon as "scientific proof".

In Seattle during the 2009-12 fiscal years, the Youth Violence Prevention Initiative budget included a multimillion dollar effort to try and change how the city dealt with youth violence. This included monitoring gang members, who commit a far higher number of crimes than your average youth, but was not exclusively limited to gang members. It was noted, youth-at-risk, gang associates, and so called Wanna-B's will often commit crimes in efforts they say will protect themselves, or to impress older Original Gangsters (OGs), or so that other youth will fear them. The Initiative serves about 800 young people a year who are at highest risk of perpetuating violence or becoming victims.

In 2008, five teenagers were shot to death in Seattle, then-Mayor Greg Nickels brought together community leaders, principals, members of the faith community, and others to develop a new approach to preventing youth and gang-related violence. The program was continued under Mayor-elect Mike McGinn. Previously, the city had a "Team for Youth" program that in early years seemed to work effectively but some said had outgrown the times. Others said the change was more about youth service providers jockeying for position for government funding.

Los Angeles Mayor Antonio Villaraigosa pointed to a 17% overall reduction in gang crime since the city's new anti-gang program started, but there again stats can be skewed, and the drop in crime may not be entirely attributed to such programs. Many critics point out that gang and drug intervention programs are easily infiltrated by gang members who may use these programs as fronts. This includes the hiring of many "former" male gang members as well as hiring female staff that often are married or have boyfriends who are or were gang members. In Los Angeles, it was found that some gang intervention workers were involved in criminal activity, funding was scrapped for some programs and a new initiative was put in place. Other people say only past gang members can understand current gang members and their issues. Regardless, ever since it was implemented, there was a lot of debate over the L.A.'s expensive gang program.

In Chicago, a long tradition of gang violence surged in 2010-12. Some former gang officers stated that it was due in part to a new generation of gangsters eager to make their mark on neighborhoods. Some former Chicago Police Department staff confided that the department changed how it operated after several scandals hit the Gang Units and not always in good ways. Some officers believed CPD engaged in de-policing for fear of being investigated or wrongfully accused by gang members. They said it was best to just sit back and not be pro-active any longer. Gang crime soared! In particular, as it was pointed out, gang crime would go up when there was a gang shooting and right afterwards there was a retaliatory shooting so the crime rate doubled right there unless better efforts were made to be pro-active after a gang shooting.

The Chicago Police Department is going to "retool our gang strategy from top to bottom", said Supt. Garry McCarthy on March 19, 2012. McCarthy said the department's new strategy will include a gang audit that merges two kinds of intelligence data into a central repository for the beat officer. This effort was supported by then Chicago Mayor Rahm Emmanuel who was the former Chief of Staff for past President Barack Obama.

Meanwhile, Chicago's Cease Fire program hired former gang members as "Interrupters". The program focused on three main stages to reduce violence: 1) Identification & Detection, 2) Interruption, Intervention, & Risk Reduction, 3) Changing Behavior and Norms.

All four of these cited programs have their critics and their supporters. Again, the problems raised above often makes it very hard to tell if gang prevention and intervention programs are always effective. Still, we must try to combat gang problems in our communities. We must try to figure out how well it is working but not just rely on stats alone. Gang unit officers, youth intervention workers, gang prevention workers are the real experts when it comes to dealing with gangs. Parents and school staff are also big stakeholders.

I say survey all of them "anonymously" in the areas of Suppression, Intervention, and Prevention, because otherwise they might feel compelled to rate their success higher due to employment or funding issues, and that will likely be a good gauge if programs and agencies really work. We must also remember that it can cost $40,000 or more a year to house somebody in prison. A police officer's salary can range from $50,000 a year to nearly $100,000 in some places.

A small amount of money spent on trying to prevent and deter youth from joining gangs or time spent intervening with young people can save us all a lot as a society in the long run and give us a quality of life that money alone cannot measure.6

Unfortunately, some gang workers, some law enforcement, and some in corrections have engaged in personal politics, petty department rivalries, ego and power trips which hasn't helped matters any. When criminal justice personnel and other professions create gang-like groups, how does that look to the gang member? How can we say, "You're wrong, but we are right?" How can we be so self-righteous? I am still totally blown away sometimes at how arrogant and closed minded some people in law enforcement and corrections can be. I'm also amazed at how many in the community and how many parents still blame the system and police for so many problems. Some even seem to be enablers for criminal behavior, make excuses for kids, and try to shield them from police. I really wonder sometimes if some leaders in the community really care about long-term solutions or just want to point the finger and blame the cops?

Police are not the main reason for gangs nor can they be the only solution. Police are more like firefighters, putting out small and large fires when they occur. Police departments need to do a better job of weeding out bad cops at the beginning of the recruitment process and do a better job of recruiting bilingual-bicultural cops who understand the complex issues of the community they work in.

Corrections and the community must not be in denial about gangs either. Gangs create a large part of the disciplinary problems in jail and prison (often around 1/3rd) and are responsible for much of the violence in custody and out on the street (often over 50% of it). Corrections must come to terms with this fact and do a better job of closing the revolving door and help those who really want help to leave the gang and drug lifestyle. Ex-offenders must abide by their conditions of release or risk going back to prison. Abiding by society's rules, staying away from other felons, drugs, and gang members are a part of the conditions for freedom.

As you can see by now, dealing with gangs is a very complex problem and cannot be separated from dealing with most other issues in the criminal justice system. It takes a collaborative effort by all effected social parties involved, juvenile, probation, jails, prisons, parole, law enforcement, and the Feds to combat gangs. As I've stated many times, "There is no gang problem, there are gang problems, thus it takes multiple solutions".

There are many local, regional, state, and national gang associations which try to do just that. One of the first was the California Gang Investigator's Association headed by long-time gang specialist Sgt. Wes McBride formerly of the Los Angeles Sheriff's Office and "Operation Safe Streets". Groups like the International Latino Gang Investigator's Association also help deter gang crime and have classes for the community.

I believe we need to improve communications with more bilingual-bicultural officers. Professional groups like the "Latino Peace Officers Association" and the "Chicano Correctional Workers Association" are working hard to improve the image of peace officers and serve as good role models. I believe we need to improve the physical conditions and businesses opportunities in the barrio. I believe that new immigrants must be educated in American customs and basic law without immigrant bashing them.7

To end these problems takes positive social action over the long-term. We can't solve this tragedy in 1, 2, 5, or even ten years. It may be two full generations before we can solve it. But we must start sometime without excuses for criminal behavior. As long as some community leaders keep making excuses for any type of criminal behavior, we will not change the situation. Police and Gangsters both need to be held accountable for their actions.

You can probably tell; I take my job very seriously and at times I have been very tormented by issues discussed in this book as I contemplated how to better deal with them. I don't claim to know everything as I learn new things every day and try to improve my work in this area. I don't believe anybody out there is the sole expert.

To claim otherwise would be complete arrogance. Some of my colleagues still may think I'm a little soft but I feel while police departments have been bolstered significantly in recent years, many social programs have suffered severe cut-backs. To effectively address street gangs, we need a national and coordinated "Prevention, Intervention, and Suppression Program", not just a "Drug Czar". You can call me a social worker if you want.

Social problems are inter-related to all the problems we presently face in the criminal justice system. Ending poverty, racism, enforcing gun control, providing meaningful education and job training must accompany the tough guy policies. We need to do a better job of being pro-active and nip problems in the bud before they get out of hand. People should have an awareness of juvenile prevention and gang strategies that are working.8

We must continue to address gang violence at all levels and have more dialogue between the administration of justice system and the community. People who know me well, know that I do

Prevention, Intervention, and Suppression work. I often tell people I would like to be unemployed, unfortunately people go to jail. Ever since my 21st Birthday, on that fateful night when the first documented shooting involving Latino gang occurred in Seattle, I have worked hard to combat these problems. We still have a long way to go, but it is too important a battle to give up. When people ask me why I am so concerned about gangs, I tell them a bit about my life story.

One of many things I learned while writing this book was that members of my own family have been subject to prejudice and discrimination. I found that many people in the community had some real bad experiences dealing with cops. This also happened to me sometimes while growing up and even during the course of writing this book. In some cases, officers whom I trusted betrayed me, called me a liar, talked about me as if I was a low life in bed with thugs, undermined my work, and some of them made things personal and abused their authority.

There were also some youth workers and power brokers that criticized me because they thought I was too close to cops. Yet, this does not destroy my faith in improving the system. I know Administration of Justice work is a tough job, one that not many people are willing to do. Not all staff should be painted with the same brush.

Most that I personally know are very respectful and competent officers and I am proud to call them my friends!

Source References

CHAPTER 1

The Secret Band of Brothers 1

Jeff Green 1847

DOC Gang Handbook 2

Dennis Spice 1994

Teenage Gangs 3

Dale Kramer, Madeline Carr, Sen. Estes Kefauver

Popular Press Library 7/57

The New Ethnic Mobs 4

William Kleinkect

Free Press 1996

Gang ID & Management 5

Gabriel Morales/Sherman Wilkins

CJTC 1995

The American Street Gang 6

Malcom Klein

University of Oxford Press 1995

Chicago Police Wearily Track New Violent Gangs 7

John Dobberstein

Daily Southtown 1/17/04

Down in the Barrio 8

Joanne Moore

Temple University Press 1991

CHAPTER 2

J. Reyes Interview 12/911

Barrio Warriors 2

Gus Frias

Diaz Publications 1982

Barrio Gangs 3

James Vigil

University of Texas Press 1980

Mexican American Youth 4

Celia Heller

Random House 12/68

Richard Castruita Interview 5

Montebello, CA 12/92

The Zoot-Suit Riots 6

M. Manzon

University of Texas Press 1985

Riot Alarm sent out in Zoot War 7

L.A. Times 6/8/43

G.V. Morales Interview 8

Seattle, WA 12/94

Land of a Thousand Dances 9

David Reyes

University of New Mexico Press 1997

Andando Sangrando 10

Armando Morales

Percpectiva Publications 1972

Understanding Street Gangs 11

Robert Jackson & Wes McBride

Copperhouse Publishing 1985

A History of Gang Violence 12

LA Times 12/11/88

L.A. Lawless 13

David Ellis

Time Magazine 5/11/92

Homegirls: The Chicana Gangs 14

John C. Quicker

International University Press 1983

A Parent's Guide to Street Gangs 15

Felix Aguirre

Marin Publications 1993

Girls in Gangs 16

Virginia de Leon

Yakima Herald Republic 3/18/90

8-Ball Chicks 17

Gini Sykes

Anchor Books/Doubleday Publications 1992

A Study of 100 Female Offenders 18

G.C.Morales 2003

CHAPTER 3

Desperados 1

Elaine Shannon

Viking/Penguin Press 1988

Will Leader's Arrest Hurt Cali Cartel? 2

Seattle Times 6/11/95

Sinaloa Pays in Blood for Drug War 3

Sam Quinones

L.A. Times 2/21/99

CHAPTER 4

Progress-Bulletin 8/1/77

Chicano Inmates: The Key to San Quentin 4

Theodore Davidson 1974

Prison Gangs: Inmates Battle for Control 5

Victor Cox

Corrections Compendium 4/86

Update on Sacramento Prison Inmate Disturbance 6

CDC New Release 10/3/96

21 in NF Prison Gang Indicted 7

San Jose-Mercury News 6/3/92

Nuestra Familia Prison Gang not as deadly as it has been 8

Sandra Gonzales

San Jose Mercury News 10/23/94

Combating Gangs in Texas 9

Sam Buentello

Corrections Today Magazine 7/92

From Carnalismo to Chaos 10

Steve Lucero, Gabe Morales

Amazon/KDP 2014

CHAPTER 5

Mara Salvatrucha, Eighteenth Street
and Sureno Gangs Across America 1

Andy Eways, Gabe Morales

Police & Fire Publishing

Rafael Cancio Interview 2

Portland, OR 10/98

Gang Related Shootings on Officers 3

Dan Nalian

West Covina PD 1995

An Inside Look at the 18th Street Menace 4

Rich Connell and Robert Lopez

L.A. Times 11/17/96

Salvadoran Refugees find new Civil War in L.A. 5

Peter Hect

L.A. Times 12/6/91

Seattle PD Ed Harris Interview 6

Seattle, WA 12/96

The History of the Nuestra Familia 7

Gabe Morales

Amazon/KDP 2013

Statesville - The Penitentiary for Mass Society 8

James Jacobs

University of Chicago Press 1975

Sherman Wilkins Interview 9

Seattle, WA 11/96

CHAPTER 6

Concrete Mama 1

John McCoy

University of Missouri Press 1981

Gang Interviews 2-15

1992-2012

CHAPTER 7

Latino Gangster Rap-Article 1

G.C. Morales 2000

Latino Gangster Rap-Article 2

G.C. Morales 2006

Latino Gangster Rap-Article 3

G.C. Morales 2008

Latino Music 4

Gabe Morales

Amazon/KDP 2016

CHAPTER 8

The Evolution of Street Gangs 1

Michael McCort

The Police Chief April 1998

Family Drug Bust in Ontario 2

Daily Bulletin 9/18/98

"Drug Overdose Statistics" 3

Seattle Department of Public Health 1997-2011

Dr. J. Amador Interview 4

Seattle, WA 2/99

L.A. County Gang Homicide Rates 5

LASO 1997

Juvenile Offenders and Victims 6

U.S. Department of Justice 1996

"Killer Costs: Guns, Money and Medicine" 7

Erik Freeland

U.S. News 7/1/96

For Teens, Illegal Guns easy to get on Street 8

Casey McNerthney

Seattle P-I 9/1/08

Gang and Guns in Washington State 9

Enrique Cerna

KCTS Ch. 9 Connects 2/4/11

CHAPTER 9

Classification and Security Threat Management 1

G.C. Morales 1993-2016

CHAPTER 10

Veterano Interview 1

Pomona, CA 12/92

Rising above Gangs and Drugs 2

Natalie Salazar

L.A. Community Reclamation Project News 9/10/90

Gangs in Direct Supervision 3

Gabriel Morales

WSJA Magazine 1999

Father Greg Boyle Interview 4

East L.A. 5/99

José Gallegos Interview 5

Azuza, CA 5/99

Delfino Muñoz Interview 6

Seattle, WA 12/98

Albino Garcia Interview 7

Yakima, WA, 2000

Cook Barrett Interview 8

Albany, NY, 2012

The Impact of Gang Membership 9

G. David Curry and Scott Decker

University of Missouri Press 7/95

Inmate Daily Reports 10

King County Jail 1994-2012

Gang Enforcement through Saturation, Patrol,

Aggressive Curfew, and Truancy Enforcement 11

Fritsch, T. Caeti, R. Taylor

Crime and Delinquency Journal

Sage Publications Jan. 1999

Official Seeks Injunction against 92 Gang Members 12

Jeffery Rabin

L.A. Times 5/4/98

Bulging Prisons Creates more Friction 13

Seattle P-I 12/18/98

Inmate Assault Rate 14

CDC 1995

Chapter 11

Cops, Crooks and Politicians 1

Neil W. Moloney

Peanut Butter Publishing 1994

Secret Clique in L.A. County Sheriff's Gang Unit Probed 2

Robert Faturechi

Los Angeles Times 4/20/12

State Prison Guards hold their Firepower 3

Sacramento Bee 1/30/99

National Law Enforcement Officers Memorial 4

2011/2021 Statistics

SPD Louie Olivarez Interview 5

Seattle, WA 1/99

Gangsters, Cops, and Politicians Blog 6

Gang Prevention Services 4/12

Hispanics Learning Basics of American Law 7

Joseph Rose Yakima Herald Republic 8/30/96

Youth Gang Prevention Efforts Are Taking Hold 8

Michelle Gaseau

Corrections Connection 12/14/98

Acknowledgments

I would like to thank the following people who have helped me in my career, personal development, and my life and have contributed in some way to the realization of this book:

Ruby Aguilar, Felix Aguirre, Dr. Julio Amador, Nelson Arriaga, Tony Avendorph, Bernal Baca, Mike Barigian, Cook Barrett, John Barrios, Vergel Bautista, Kenneth Bell, Robert Belshay, Juan Borrego, Imelda Bottemly, Father Greg Boyle, Carlos Bratcher, P.J. Braun, Fae Brooks, Sam Buentello, Rafael Cancio, Carmen Carreón, Marylou Carrillo, Enrique Cerna, Roberto Cepeda, George Chavez, Dan Connors, Eduardo Cordero, Dave Cortez, Guillermo Cravens, Wes Dailey Jr., Charlie Davis, Dave Deach, Todd DePalma, Adrian Diaz, Ricardo Diaz, Steve Duncan, Bill Dunn, Al Durr, Louie Duran, "Rocky" Dyer, Magdalena Escobar, Marc Espinoza, Keith Evans, Andrew Eways, Joe Gagliardi, Adrian Garcia, Juan Garcia, José Gallegos, Greg Garner, Emil Garza, Gary Garza, Rey Garza, Chris Grant, Ben Griego, Joe Guzmán. Rick "Cowboy" Handel, Harry Hansen, Rod Hardin, Ed Harris, Sheila Hatch, La Mar Hudson, Tony Kail, T.J. Leyden, Mariko Lockhart, Steve Lucero, Tagaloa Manu, Frank "Paco" Marcell, Pablo Martinez, Rosa Melendez, Wes McBride, Laura McKeown, Joe Melone, Dave Miranda, Mario Molina, Jeri Moomaw, Tony Moreno, Adrian Moroles, Delfino Muñoz, Claudia Murphy, George Norris, Louie Olivarez, Robert Ornleas, Aida Orozco, Felipe Ortiz, Jim Ortiz, Criccy Pelayo, Joe Preciado, Jesse Quintero, Jesse Rangel, Brad Richmond, David Rodriguez, Marlene Rodriguez, Jesse Ruelas, Claudio Saa, Joe Salazar, Olga Sanchez, Edwin Santana, Lou Savelli, Chuck Schoville, Dennis Spice, Ramon Suarez, Dora Trevino, "T.K.O." Villareal, Aurora Torres, Richard Valdemar, Al Valdez, Bill Valentine, Ray Verdugo, Jesus Villahermosa, Susan Villajaro, Dale Welling, David White, Sherman Wilkins, Orlando Ybarra, and especially to: Robert "Moco" Morrill